ENGAGED

PAT DELUHERY
AND **THE GOLDEN AGE** OF DEMOCRATIC PARTY ACTIVISM

Pat Deluhery
with Steve Dunn

Copyright © 2020 by Pat Deluhery

All rights reserved. No part of this book may be reproduced or transmitted in any form or by any means, electronic or mechanical, including photocopying, recording or by any information storage and retrieval system, without written permission of the publisher.

ISBN 978-0-578-58313-6 (softbound)
ISBN 978-0-578-58315-0 (e-book)

First published in 2020 by Patrick J. Deluhery.
629 Foster Drive
Des Moines, IA 50312

Front cover photo by Steve Dunn.

Cover design by Kirstin Martin, Rae Design, rae.design.

Book design by Kirstin Martin, Rae Design, rae.design.

Interior photos courtesy of Pat Deluhery.

Edited by Pat Deluhery, Mardi Deluhery, Steve Dunn, Dan Looker, Jeff Dunn, and Paula Barbour.

Printed and distributed by IngramSpark, ingramspark.com.

PAT DELUHERY TIMELINE

1942 — **January 31, 1942:** Born in Birmingham, Alabama to Frank and Lucille (Donovan) Deluhery.

1945 — **1945:** Moves to Donovan family farm near Bernard, Iowa with family.

1947 — **1947:** Moves to Davenport, Iowa with family.

1956 — **1956:** Finishes elementary school at St. Paul the Apostle in Davenport.

1960 — **1960:** Graduates from Davenport Assumption High School in Davenport.

1964 — **1964:** Graduates with honors from the University of Notre Dame in South Bend, Indiana.

1967 — **1967:** Graduates with honors from London School of Economics in London, England.

August 1967 to May 1968: Economics instructor at St. Ambrose College in Davenport.

1968

May 25, 1968: Begins working for Iowa Gov. Harold Hughes' campaign for U.S. Senate.

1969

January 1969 to 1975: Works as legislative assistant in Hughes' Senate office in Washington, D.C.

1973

1973: Marries Margaret (Mardi) Morris in Washington, D.C.

1975

January to July 1975: Works for U.S. Sen. John Culver of Iowa in Washington, D.C. and then rejoins St. Ambrose University as an assistant professor of economics and business administration.

1978

November 7, 1978: Elected to Iowa Senate from a Scott County, Iowa district; continues teaching economics and business during the summer session and fall semester through 2001.

2002

December 2002: Resigns from Iowa Senate after unsuccessful run for statewide office in November 2002.

2007

2007: Retires from the executive branch of Iowa state government.

2019

2019: Writes memoirs with retired journalist Steve Dunn of Des Moines.

CONTENTS

	Forward	6
1	1968	10
2	Early life	25
3	High school years	35
4	Notre Dame days	43
5	Off to London	57
6	Land college job	65
7	Bobby, MLK Jr., and me	71
8	Ida Grove event	76
9	Office issue	81
10	Let's not forget Park	94
11	Nixon under fire	97
12	Secret air war	106
13	The perfect woman	109
14	Move back to Iowa	116
15	Juggling act	125
16	'78 State Senate bid	130
17	Landmark legislation	137
18	19th century Iowa becomes 20th century Iowa	152
	Acknowledgments	169
	Author bios	172

FORWARD

When I found out that Pat Deluhery had worked in U.S. Sen. Harold Hughes' office in Washington, D.C. at the height of the Vietnam War and had served in the Iowa Senate for twenty-four years, I knew there was a story to tell. And the more I inquired about his time in the nation's and state's capitals, my beliefs were confirmed: He had a story that would resonate with the general public, not just his family and friends.

The timing of Pat's book couldn't be better, either. As I write this, more than a dozen Democratic candidates are crisscrossing Iowa in hopes of winning the first-in-the-nation Iowa caucuses on February 3, 2020.

Pat's story is a story typical of the Irish Catholic, labor union experience of the early- and mid-twentieth century. His father had an eighth grade education, yet played an important role in wiring the new Alcoa plant in Davenport, Iowa in the late 1940s and early 1950s and eventually owned his own electrical business. Coincidentally, the union membership rate in the U.S. hit an all-time low of 10.5 percent in 2018. Except for the 2008 financial crisis, the rate has been declining since the 1980s, when the share of organized labor was approximately twice what it is today.

After graduating from parochial high school in Davenport, Pat attended and graduated from the University of Notre Dame in South Bend, Indiana where he benefitted from iconic instructors and was immersed in the university's social justice message with a worldview as articulated by President Theodore Hesburgh. Taking advice "that you should do whatever you feel like doing," Pat then studied at the London School of Economics in London, England just as the Vietnam War ramped up, the civil rights movement culminated with the passage of the Civil Rights Act of 1964, and more and more women entered the workforce.

Only twenty-six years old at the time, Pat got his first taste of elective politics at the national level no less. As an integral part of Iowa Gov. Harold Hughes' campaign for the U.S. Senate in 1968, Pat was introduced to retail politics at its best, setting up Hughes' appearances as an advance man.

Once Pat got to Washington, D.C. in 1969, he was an eyewitness to some of the most significant events of the late 1960s and early 1970s: a letter from the son of constituents describing the secret bombing by U.S. forces outside Vietnam; the passage of Hughes' landmark legislation dealing with alcohol and drug addiction; anti-Vietnam War marches; Hughes' decision to support Eugene McCarthy rather than Hubert Humphrey for the Democratic presidential nomination in 1968; and the formation of the Midwest Caucus of Democratic Senators, which included the likes of Humphrey, Walter Mondale, Stuart Symington, Adlai Stevenson III, and Birch Bayh.

Along the way, Pat vividly recounts experiences with an insider's insight: a benefit for Hughes in Ida Grove, Iowa in December 1968; a campaign event for Lt. Gov. Bob Fulton at the Sioux City, Iowa stockyards in 1970; a conversation between Hughes and congressman John Culver in 1971; plane rides to and from Des Moines, Iowa with Sens. Mike Mansfield, Edmund Muskie, and Stuart Symington in 1973; and an appearance by Sen. Ted Kennedy in Sioux City in 1974.

Pat's time in the Iowa Senate was just as noteworthy. He played a major role in the passage of historic pieces of legislation dealing with groundwater protection, waste reduction and recycling, and energy efficiency. With climate change accelerating and Iowa's water still struggling with excess nitrates, Pat's work is more important than ever, says journalist Dan Looker, who reviewed the book's manuscript before publication.

Pat also makes a valuable contribution with his take on how nineteenth century Iowa became twentieth century Iowa. Not only was the Hawkeye state slow to reapportion after a 1962 U.S. Supreme Court decision, but also it was slow to react to the end of Prohibition. Nevertheless, the state set up community college districts during Hughes' tenure as governor in the 1960s. It also increased the amount of state funding for public education at the K-12 level.

Although I didn't meet Pat until five years ago, I feel I've known him much longer than that. I share his interest in politics; though I've never sought political office, I've covered a lot of candidates and officeholders as a newspaper reporter and managing editor for decades before retiring in 2014. In fact, his recollection of Democratic U.S. Senate candidate Dick Clark walking across Iowa in 1972 brought to mind Democratic gubernatorial candidate Dan Walker's walk across Illinois when I was a cub reporter fresh out of college in 1971.

And how could I not identify with Pat's recounting of his days in Sen. Hughes' office in D.C. during the turbulent 1960s? I was a student at Bradley University in Peoria, Illinois then, majoring in journalism and taking several political science courses as an unofficial minor. I can remember at least one anti-war march down the main street past the Bradley campus. I also recall hearing the news about the shooting by National Guard troops at Kent State University in Ohio. Pat's recollections of Hughes supporting McCarthy after initially leaning toward Robert Kennedy and Humphrey for the Democratic presidential nomination in 1968 also hit home. I was one of the Bradley students who took a bus to Indiana one weekend to knock on doors and try to drum up support for McCarthy. Unfortunately for McCarthy, I got a tepid reception from the mostly conservative populace in the Hoosier state, a state I had once lived in.

As an Iowa native by way of Clarinda, I was fascinated when Pat described how nineteenth century Iowa became twentieth century Iowa. Although I left Iowa when my father graduated from Iowa State College in 1951, I remember my father and mother talking about growing up in the Hawkeye state in the 1920s, 1930s, and 1940s.

I was also struck by Pat's family lineage. As I noted before, his father, Frank, wired the new Alcoa plant in Davenport in the late 1940s and early 1950s. At one time, my father and two of his older brothers worked for the aluminum company at the same time. None of them ever worked at the Davenport plant, though.

Now, how did we get to this point? I started recording Pat's recollections in October 2018. After each session, I transcribed the oral version onto paper. After sixteen "chapters" were put on paper in June, former Meredith Corp. employee Dan Looker reviewed the raw manuscript and offered suggestions, including using chronological order rather than a thematic approach. With that in mind, I reworked the text, which involved a lot of cutting and pasting.

Next, Pat reviewed the updated manuscript, which had expanded to eighteen chapters by this time. After I reworked the manuscript again, Pat and his wife, Mardi, looked the final manuscript over to ensure their suggestions had been implemented. Jeff Dunn, culture critic, writer, educator, and, full disclosure, my brother, provided valuable feedback. Paula Barbour, a content editor for *Successful Farming* magazine, added her editing expertise before publication. And last, but certainly not least, graphic designer Kirstin Martin of K RAE Design laid out the book using self-publishing tools.

Yes, *Engaged: Pat Deluhery and the Golden Age of Democratic Party Activism* is more than a family history. It's a fascinating look at life in the U.S. in the 1940s and 1950s from an Irish Catholic family's perspective, the national political landscape in the 1960s and 1970s, and Iowa state government from 1978 to 2002. Finally, the title, which was suggested by my brother, comes from Looker's observation that the book describes "the golden age of Democratic Party activism," inspired by the Kennedys and advanced by Harold Hughes as Iowa governor and U.S. senator.

I hope you enjoy reading Pat's – and America's – story as much as I did putting it together for him.

Steve Dunn

CHAPTER 1

1968

HUGHES-FOR-SENATE campaign launches Deluhery's career in politics.

So I had a job on Gov. Harold Hughes' campaign staff as early as that Friday night, May 31. It's unforgettable. I was on the eighth floor of the Savery Hotel in Des Moines at about 5 o'clock at the Harold Hughes-for-Senate campaign headquarters. Campaign coordinator Ed Campbell was dealing with all kinds of issues.

Ed said to me, "You wait here. I have to deal with something else."

So Steve Delaney, who was a funeral director in Clinton, Iowa said, "Let me pour you a drink."

I said, "No, I'm not going to drink." The bottle had a label that said, "This bottle belongs to Tom Mulgrew. Do not touch."

He said, "I understand you're going to work for the governor."

That was in a sense my first confirmation.

And I said, "Perhaps. I haven't had that conversation yet, and it hasn't been confirmed."

He said, "I'm on the funeral licensing board, you know. I really hope the governor reappoints me."

And I said, "Really? Why do you say that?"

He looked at me like … I was so naïve. He said, "Well, I enjoy the work."

Those appointments mean so much for so many people. In fact, they count something for me even today. For Steve Delaney from Clinton, this was a very big deal. It gave him standing among all the other funeral directors from around the state. There were three people on the board.

I learned from him that if there is an alcohol-related incident with a funeral director, the licensing board has to deal with it. They can't have licensed funeral directors crashing the vehicles. For me it was one of those early lessons of what politics and this kind of stuff is really like. It relates to a federal system because it's the kind of thing that's done at the state level. What's important in one state is not so important in another state.

Anyway, I went back to Davenport, Iowa to St. Ambrose College for graduation that Sunday afternoon. That's the weekend that started the rest of my adult life. Ed Campbell wanted me to come back on Monday morning.

I said, "I can't. I've got to close out this small apartment I'm in. I'll come back Tuesday morning."

He said, "Fine."

So I drove back to Des Moines on Tuesday morning.

The people at the St. Ambrose graduation knew I was going to work for the Hughes campaign the next day. So the question at the graduation was, "Are you going to write position papers for Gov. Hughes?"

I'd say, "Well, no, not really."

What I actually ended up doing was setting up picnics. We did forty-six picnics in five weeks.

I staffed the picnics as the advance man. Later, *advance man* became a buzzword. Several authors wrote about their careers as advance men. At the time, it was just an assignment.

The task was to engage with the Harold Hughes network in a way that invited nice, friendly, instant communication from them to me back in Des Moines. And that happened. Again, I couldn't define it that way at that time. But that's what Campbell hired me for. If you relate to these people and they relate to you, then we keep our finger on the pulse of what's going on around the state. And that proved to be the case because in those days you had just two phone lines into the headquarters. People had a hard time getting through.

The advantage I had in the campaign for U.S. senator as a low-level staff guy was that Hughes had already been governor for six years. So there were ample people around who wanted to be associated with him. There were all these appointees to the boards and commissions. That first day when I met Tom Mulgrew, a businessman and prominent Democrat from Dubuque, Iowa, Delaney, and others, it was obvious to me that this won't be hard if I get the job. And then I got the job that day.

I was a low-level staff guy. I was twenty-six years old. At the time it didn't strike me, but I've thought since then about Park Rinard, who was the director of the Iowa League of Municipalities, coming over and having lunch with Ed Campbell and me at the hotel. I didn't realize it at the time, but that was my job interview with Park for the work I did the next six years.

Another guy who came for lunch was John Chrystal who, at the time, was state bank superintendent. John Chrystal's mother was a Garst. The Garsts and Chrystal were players in the world of Iowa politics, Democratic politics, state government, and international relations. When Nikita Kruschev, the premier of the Soviet Union, came to Iowa in 1959, he visited the Garsts' family farm. Nonetheless, Chrystal was interested in me. He knew the bankers in Davenport. We had lived in Davenport since about 1947. My father first had been a superintendent on a job for Alcoa and then he started Deluhery Electric. I knew the bankers in Davenport, too, especially the Figges. So John always found it entertaining talking with me about banks and banking families and all of that.

Four weeks before I met Campbell, Delaney, and others at the campaign headquarters at the Savery Hotel, I had an interview in the governor's office. Dwight Jensen asked, "Have you studied public administration?"

I said, "No, I haven't. I studied economics, politics, and a little bit of sociology. I was an English major at Notre Dame. It was all about the stories."

Paul Ryan in Davenport was the one who made a phone call to Ed Campbell to say, "Pat Deluhery has applied for a job in the Hughes campaign. Take a look at him. He would be good." That's what got me the interview with Ed Campbell and Dwight Jensen in the governor's office that spring of 1968, and then I was hired.

After I joined the campaign staff in May 1968, Ed Campbell took me up to the statehouse for a personal visit with Gov. Hughes. This was about a week after I came on board. We talked about the campaign effort with the governor for a few minutes. Then Ed and I walked back downtown to the Hotel Savery. Ed said to me, "Harold Hughes will say things and do things which seem to run directly counter to his election chances. But they have a way of working out. And in the end, he's stronger."

I watched Harold Hughes, the candidate, confirm this impression in the campaign of '68 and during his six years in the U.S. Senate.

For example, young people made many older citizens feel uneasy during the summer of '68. Gov. Hughes championed their cause. "I'm more concerned about long faces on adults," he said, "than long hair and beards on their children."

Another example: Two assassinations that year, of Martin Luther King Jr. and Robert F. Kennedy, caused people to wonder whether domestic order could be preserved. This caused candidates around the country to steer clear of controversy. Gov. Hughes took a different course, using his position to call on Iowans to make our state a model for the nation in race relations.

Gov. Hughes organized a series of "Crisis Conferences" around the state with the help of religious leaders from all faiths. My dad and I attended the one in Davenport at Assumption High School. The Catholic bishop, an African American Methodist bishop, other religious leaders, and Gov. Hughes spoke. The message was "Iowa does not have a large minority community. So we should be a model for the nation."

About three weeks after I was hired to work on the Hughes-for-Senate campaign, we did our first five-day run on Tuesday, Wednesday, Thursday, Friday, and Saturday. We'd get the candidate, Gov. Hughes, back to Des Moines by late Saturday afternoon or evening. The first day out was Adel, Guthrie Center, Audubon, and Carroll. So first we'd lay out a breakfast, then twenty-four miles away, mid-morning coffee, and then another twenty-four miles for lunch. We'd drive in the afternoon, have a break, and get Hughes in a hotel with his wife, daughter, and driver who drove the Winnebago camper. Then we'd do an evening event in Carroll.

We had another guy who was paid for by the United Auto Workers whose name was Mel Gioffredi. Mel drove the car, but Ed made it clear to me the first day "it's not Mel's job to deal with these people." He was so urban, so Des Moines, and so union. It seemed better for him to keep a low profile – he knew that, too. He'd be quiet and have me do the talking with people. Mel and I would ride together in a station wagon that was painted with "Harold Hughes for U.S. Senate" on it. The governor; his wife, Eva; their daughter, Phyllis, who was about sixteen years old then; the driver; and Ed Campbell would be in the Winnebago camper.

Mel and I would be out ahead by an hour or so. Once we got one event going, we'd go to the next one. We did that Tuesday through Saturday. Then we took a couple of weeks off. We'd advance the next two weeks and did the same thing Tuesday through Saturday. We did all that up to about the point of the Democratic Convention in Chicago August 26-29, 1968.

There was a lot for me to learn and do, and I enjoyed it immensely. On the first day out, we had a reporter named Alan Otten from the *Wall Street Journal*. He rode in the camper with Hughes. Even though I was doing this job on picnics and planning, I knew Otten more than most others on the team because I had been reading the *Wall Street Journal* for ten years.

Another person who came to work on the campaign was Gov. Hughes' Aunt Esther. So Ed set them up; we were on the eighth floor of the Hotel Savery. You needed a statewide headquarters starting Labor Day. Aunt Esther and Sam Brown were at the headquarters. Sam was a national leader of young people in the McCarthy presidential campaign. He grew up in Council Bluffs and later was elected to a statewide office in Colorado.

Anyway, as many as sixty young people who had worked in the McCarthy campaign came, too. We didn't pay for them. Sam had arranged payment and how they slept. It wasn't our problem. Aunt Esther and Sam would tangle. She would count all the pencils and Sam would spend money like it was going out of style.

David Stanley was our opponent in the U.S. Senate race in 1968. Stanley had announced against the incumbent Republican U.S. senator, Bourke Hickenlooper, prior to the end of 1967. Hickenlooper was a four-term, twenty-four-year U.S. senator from Iowa, and he'd been governor for four years before that. Hickenlooper had been in office since 1940. He had had a very distinguished career on the Senate Foreign Relations Committee, and he was a real player in Washington.

Hughes did not announce anything until December 1967. My mother saw me reading the clipping of the announcement by Hughes. She said, "Maybe you ought to try to go work for a guy like him." And I said, "Yeah, I'm thinking about it." Stanley was the son of Max Stanley of Muscatine. There was a family in Davenport called the Walshes who ran the Walsh Construction Company. Max Stanley ran a small engineering company in Muscatine. The Walshes brought Max Stanley into the modern world, so to speak. The Walshes worked on the job that led to the opening of Lake Michigan to ocean-going vessels, the St. Lawrence Seaway, during the Eisenhower administration. It interested me at the time as a young person in Davenport. John F. Kennedy had supported that project despite the wishes of the Massachusetts port.

The Walshes were Irish, Catholic, and Democrats, but they had supported Eisenhower in the last two weeks of the 1952 presidential campaign. My dad was surprised. They thought Eisenhower would win, so they'd better be on the right side of this one.

Max Stanley had followed the Walshes, and he also got some work on the St. Lawrence Seaway; that established Stanley Consultants, which exists to this day in Muscatine. So their son, David, was this stellar figure in the family. We always understood that he was at the top of his class at the University of Iowa and the University of Iowa Law School and undoubtedly widely connected. David was elected to the Iowa General Assembly.

Hickenlooper got out of the race in January 1968 after Hughes announced in December. He had served four terms as a U.S. senator and two terms as Iowa's governor. He was a very talented man. I met Hickenlooper during the summer of 1960, but I was not as respectful of Hickenlooper as most of the people around Hughes. I think he had voted in the Senate against the Marshall Plan and the Peace Corps. That's how I viewed him. But other people might say that's a very narrow approach to Hickenlooper.

David had to win a big three-way primary on the Republican side for U.S. senator. By summertime, David was their nominee, having won the Republican primary. There was one particular sign I remember that said "Nixon Needs Stanley" and then somebody had written underneath it "But America Needs Hughes." When that was discovered, pictures were taken of it, which we used a lot around the state. Different Democrats loved it. We had people supporting us like the lieutenant governor and others who would work it into their speeches.

The ballot in 1968 included not only the president, but also U.S. senator. At that time, Iowa had six or seven congressmen. Then you had all the statewide offices, state legislature, and county elected officials. In those days, the governor and statewide offices were elected every two years, so 1968 was a huge political year. Our events during those four weeks I described were opportunities for all kinds of candidates and officeholders to gather. I didn't realize it at the time, but it was immensely important to my future. In one sense, I was in charge of the event. Ed Campbell had a role and the county chair had a role, but I was the one who pulled the trigger.

The Democratic Party in Iowa in 1968 was still a party that did not have the support of the Protestant elite of Iowa. Democrats had the Garsts and lots of people who were rich and did a lot of things. But when you went from county to county, especially in small town and rural Iowa, the county chair and three or four people who put the event together were almost always Irish and Catholic. They could put an event together and draw a lot of other people to it, but it led Ed Campbell to say to me, "I told Dwight Jensen you take to this like a duck takes to water." That meant I could relate to the local Democrats even though I was from Davenport and had gone to Notre Dame and London, which separated me in some ways from a lot of people.

Nonetheless, I could relate to my cousins in Bernard and Cascade, Iowa on the far edge of Dubuque County and to all those small towns. It wasn't hard for me at all. It was just like going into Cascade and Bernard.

Ed Campbell explained his work this way: We work hard with each strand and then blend them all together. We have all these strands – the young people, labor union people, teachers, and others. And then you work them all together, giving each of them their own identity at the end.

In the labor movement, the UAW had a very hard-working, distinguished guy named Idris "Soapy" Owens. We had a man named Hugh Donovan Clark, who was the head of the AFL-CIO in Iowa. It turned out that Clark was an old friend of my dad's, and he was a distant cousin of my mother's. Under the surface, the Democratic Party in Iowa had this huge flavor of eastern Iowa and people I could connect with.

Over in Davenport in 1968 we had a similar headquarters with Bill Gluba, my classmate, later mayor of Davenport and a state senator. Gluba was kind of an uneasy fit with Paul Ryan, my father's friend, to run the Harold Hughes operation in Scott County. Bill would spend money like it was going out of style while Paul would try to hold him down. Anyway, it was a delicate balancing act with the traditional Democrats around the state, many of them officeholders and certainly the county chairs, who were at least forty years old. Campbell was just an artist in this. There was the enthusiasm and willingness to work with the young people, who were idealistic.

Hughes had taken a stand against the war in Vietnam without alienating the establishment in Iowa. The North Vietnamese had the ability to send four or five or ten troops every time we killed ten troops. They had an endless supply of soldiers to overcome whatever devastation we could do. So we're not going to win the war. It's a matter of when we're going to end it. Hughes didn't talk to me at great length about those kinds of issues. He'd open up some times. The war in Vietnam was a huge issue in America.

My part, which I didn't understand at the time very clearly, was to bridge the gap between the traditional older people who were well known to Hughes and knew him and supported him, and the younger people. Hughes, Park, and Campbell could all see this, I think, and then I saw it later when we were in Washington, D.C. The young people felt abused. The discussion went on for the next fifty years that the baby boomers were so different from the forty-year-olds and sixty-year-olds who had come through the Depression and had felt grateful that we had stuff like new public schools and the interstate highway system. The baby boomers took it for granted ... *Yes, you did it all for us, and you should have.*

I was born in 1942 so I'm a bit ahead of the baby boomers, but I was young enough to relate to them. My brother was born in 1944, and my sister was born in 1949.

Hughes' inclination was to support Hubert Humphrey for the Democratic nomination for president in 1968. They had been friends for eight years or more. Humphrey had campaigned for him as far back as the 1962 election for governor. Hughes tried and tried to get Humphrey to take steps back from President Lyndon Johnson in terms of the war, but he couldn't get Humphrey to do it. Nobody else could, either. Johnson was adamant, and Humphrey knew how much pressure Johnson was under. In the end, one of the things Ed Campbell said to the McCarthy activists in Iowa was: "You don't want to make a fuss at these Hughes events. Come with your McCarthy pins and stuff and just show up. If Hughes sees people at these events around the state who are polite and supporting McCarthy, that's all you need to do."

In my job of advancing these things, I'd be at the event a half hour ahead of Hughes and the county chairs would say, "A bunch of people have shown up that we don't know. We hope they're not here to make trouble." It was a delicate balancing act.

I think Hughes was making a calculated decision that this is the way he had to go regarding the war in Vietnam. He only decided a week or two before the national convention. If Hubert wouldn't change, then Hughes would endorse McCarthy, he decided. And he did endorse McCarthy, offered to nominate McCarthy, and McCarthy accepted.

Hughes was eight years younger than Park Rinard. Hughes was a very big man. He played the tuba. There was a tragedy in his life that doesn't get mentioned much. He had an older brother; the two of them were named "Big Pack" and "Little Pack," and he was "Little Pack." His brother was killed in a car accident in the early days of auto traffic.

If anything, being a recovered alcoholic like Hughes figures pretty well in the Hughes story. Being a recovered alcoholic would be sort of valued and not exactly celebrated, but alcoholism was not unknown in the peer group of my parents and grandparents. In the '80s and '90s I had friends my age who had undergone rehabilitation as an alternative to going to jail. So in that sense, it was admired. I remember my dad saying to me during the '68 campaign, "You know, most guys who have that in their past – alcoholism and then recovery – don't want to talk about it. And for Hughes, it's almost like an advantage. He's celebrated for having come through bad times."

You know, it was all related to World War II and his horrendous wartime experiences. Just after Labor Day, somebody wrote a critical piece on Hughes. Hughes was compared unfavorably to other World War II veterans who had returned home and not become alcoholics, who made positive contributions right off the bat instead of leading ragged lives for four or five years. I was very conscious of that.

On occasion, Hughes told me that when he was in World War II, he was given a job that meant a lot more to the people who lived during that time. He was a Browning automatic rifleman. They gave that job to great big guys because they had to carry a big, heavy rifle. He had lived through at least one situation where he was in a company of twelve or fourteen soldiers and all the rest of them were killed. He survived by lying on the ground; when he got back up, no one else was alive around him. That gets portrayed in movies of D-Day to this day or movies made in the '50s, '60s, '70s, and '80s. Occasionally he would say to me, "You know, you start to blame yourself for being alive, and you're thinking, why did I get past this and nobody else around me did?"

In that way Hughes was quite profound. He was not highly educated. He had only gone one semester to the University of Iowa to play football and dropped out. He was kind of wild as an Ida Grove, heavy drinking, young guy who went to the war, got married, and had a couple of kids.

There were so many people up in northwest Iowa who could not believe that Hughes had been governor for six years. He said, "When I announced for commerce commissioner in 1958, it was the biggest joke in Ida Grove, Iowa that they'd had in years. They all thought it was just hilarious. Harold Hughes is running for the statewide position of commerce commissioner."

The Eugene McCarthy/Hubert Humphrey saga happened around the Iowa state convention, which wasn't long after Bobby Kennedy's death. In those days there were two conventions. One was called the statutory convention, which was in May, and then the state presidential convention a couple of weeks later when you chose your delegates. Both Humphrey and McCarthy came to Iowa for the second one. I was staffing that for Hughes, and we did an event on one of Bill Knapp's farms. The event was a fundraiser for some of Hughes' supporters around the state. Both of those guys – Humphrey and McCarthy – came to the fundraiser, a picnic. The convention was going on at Veterans Auditorium in Des Moines.

At the statutory convention in Iowa, Campbell told the McCarthy people that Hughes would support McCarthy. I did not go to the Chicago Democratic Convention in 1968. After the Chicago convention Ed Campbell brought a bunch of McCarthy backers to Iowa. They were the young people led by Sam Brown.

It was early in the summer of 1968 when I got to know Tom and Ruth Harkin. They'd only been married less than a year when I met them. Tom was two years older than me. When I got hired by the Hughes campaign in early June 1968, I was living in the campaign headquarters in the Hotel Savery in Des Moines. I was on the eighth floor in Room 802; I could sleep there because it was a hotel suite. Ed Campbell put me there. He said, "You can just stay here in this room." I had to get up and get dressed in the morning and all of that. Tom and Ruth, his new bride, were living on the seventh floor. They were working for the Paul Franzenburg-for-governor campaign. So I became friends with Tom and Ruth. What a career he had – ten years in the U.S. House of Representatives and thirty years as a U.S. senator.

Dan Miller was a good friend of mine. Miller finished high school in 1968 in Des Moines when I was going to work for the Harold Hughes Senate campaign. His father, Marty Miller, was the head of the Associated Press in Des Moines. Marty Miller died in the summer of 1968. So his funeral was put on the schedule for Gov. Hughes as if it were a campaign event. It clearly was not a campaign event, but Gov. Hughes really liked him and, in a political sense, was indebted to him.

As head of the AP, Marty Miller had accompanied Gov. Hughes on at least two overseas trade missions, which Hughes had done during his governorship from 1963 to 1968. Hughes knew Marty Miller very well and there were other people around Hughes who were very connected with the press such as Park Rinard, the head of the Iowa League of Municipalities, and Dwight Jensen, a former newspaperman and chief of staff in the governor's office.

I remember staffing the funeral. I did not go into the church, but I was driving the car that Hughes got into as he came out of the funeral with one or two other people. So Marty Miller's funeral played a role in my life in that late summer of 1968. His son, Dan, worked in the Hughes Senate office and later headed Iowa Public Television.

I connected with a couple of people during the '68 campaign. First, Paul Ryan, a friend of my dad's, in Davenport. I'd known him for years. Second, Cornelius "Connie" Bodine Jr. in Sioux City. He had a powerful, deep voice. He had a long background in broadcasting. Bodine had worked at a Rock Island or Moline, Illinois television station when I was ten or eleven years old. Then he had a long career of doing different jobs in the private sector as a business administrator and in meatpacking when he was in Sioux City. He conveyed Iowa meat products to restaurants in the northeast U.S. in the early to mid-1960s.

He was a very interesting person. His wife was Russian, and I've been told a grandson of his is active in politics to this day. The family has maintained a Sioux City presence for decades. At one point, Connie became business administrator of Newark, New Jersey in the 1970s and offered me a job. He asked me if I wanted to come to New Jersey and work as his assistant. I declined.

Ryan and Bodine got a very unusual call at a certain point in the 1968 campaign. And they both called me on the same day at campaign headquarters in Des Moines. The message was identical. Our campaign had said, "We have taken Harold Hughes off the campaign trail for about a week or even nine days because he got sick – the kind of sickness you'd get on a fall day. His lungs were filled with mucous and he wasn't able to speak clearly and wasn't able to campaign effectively." By then, we had campaign events scheduled. All of a sudden, instead of Hughes speaking at campaign events around the state along with statewide and local candidates, the lead speech had to be given by state Treasurer Paul Franzenburg, the Democratic candidate for governor.

But the message from Bodine and Ryan was that the main Republican supporter of our Republican opponent, David Stanley, walked up to them the morning of the call and said, "I'm sorry, Paul. I'm sorry, Connie. I know how hard you've worked for Harold Hughes and now he's let you down. He's off the wagon. They've got him sequestered. He's drunk. He's not campaigning. We know how hard you've worked to help him get elected and now he's let you down." The Hughes people would call me with that kind of stuff right away.

There are so many angles to this story. One was how hard it was to get through on the telephone. Stuff was going on all around the state. We only had a small office on the eighth floor of the Savery Hotel. There were three people in the office: Campbell, me, and one secretary. Paul and Connie thought it would be easier to get the word to me than to reach Ed Campbell or anybody in the governor's office at the state capitol. So they both called me before noon with this same message.

One of the things I learned from that was Ed Failor was trying to get our supporters to put the message out. Both Bodine and Ryan were canny enough to know that this was a setup – neither one of them would do it. Ed Failor was a former municipal judge from the 1950s in Dubuque. He had migrated into the orbit of David Stanley and the Republican establishment.

He was a resourceful, intelligent – and from our point of view, evil – campaign manager on the other side. Stanley, the opponent, was brilliant and from a very connected family in Muscatine. Failor's fingerprints would be all over these calls to Bodine and Ryan. He would have done that in less than a day. It was a big lesson to me. Later, Hughes got better and campaigned effectively around the state.

Author Vance Bourjaily and his wife hosted a big campaign event for Hughes at their Johnson County, Iowa farm. Vance was a faculty member at the Iowa Writers Workshop in Iowa City. He had written a book called *The Man Who Knew Kennedy.* He frequently rode in the campaign car with Mel and me. I've always wondered if I showed up as a comical figure in one of his later novels; I hope not with my real name.

I went to the Des Moines Hughes-Stanley debate late in the 1968 campaign down at the Savery Hotel. I was sitting in the back. They said, "We're going to control the questions so nobody gets up and asks questions, but you can write a question if you want to." I quickly took one of the pieces of paper, wrote a question, and put it in the box that they took to the front. And there were a lot of questions, and mine was among the two that were chosen to ask Stanley.

The question was, "Mr. Stanley, you say you have made mistakes and you're not afraid to admit them publicly. Can you tell us about two mistakes and what is your present position on those issues?" There was kind of a ripple of laughter across the room. And then the laughter built and they really started laughing hard. Stanley was knocked back on his heels. He looked like "this is a trick question." He broke out of that, though, by laughing and encouraging the audience to laugh.

His answer was, "Fair enough." He then mentioned two issues. One was that he'd been a member of the United World Federalists. He said, "Dwight D. Eisenhower was one of the first members of the United World Federalists, but I learned later on that's probably not a good organization for me to be associated with because there is just so much resistance to world federalism." I could see the obvious connection to his father and President Eisenhower. That clicked for me right away. The second one, he said, is capital punishment – the death penalty. He said, "When I was first elected I opposed it, but I've come to learn there are some crimes that are so brutal that there should be capital punishment."

His answer was a big enough story around the state because it undercut his critique of Hughes. He had been criticizing Hughes for his emerging critique of the war in Vietnam.

Alan Baron of Sioux City, Iowa became an enormous figure in America via the Harold Hughes campaign. He sold stocks and bonds. He probably came from a family with some money. Alan was just great. He offered to do an event about two or three weeks before Election Day at about seven-thirty in the morning at the airport in Sioux City. The goal was to raise money for last-minute expenses and encourage campaign conversation in Hughes' home territory. So we did this airport event when I was in high gear.

Mel Gioffredi and I left Des Moines probably as early as 4:45 a.m. to be up there and advance the event. When we get to the Sioux City airport, Alan is pulling them in. It's 7:15 and the boss is going to arrive on the plane by 7:30. By that time, Campbell and I were really in the groove so if he said he's going to land at 7:30, I could count on that. Hughes wanted things to be done precisely. He couldn't stand the idea of making people wait two hours. So at about 7:25, I said, "Let's go out and greet the governor when he comes in." It was kind of cold. Sure enough, the plane comes right in.

By then, I knew what it was like. These guys all want to be the one who's greeting Hughes as he comes in. They more or less tangled with each other to be first. But Hughes needed that because he was kind of shy. If we'd had them all back in the hangar or airport lounge, and he'd have had to walk across the tarmac, it wouldn't have been the event it was. When he came down those little steps, he fell into the crowd, and they all wanted to be the first one to shake his hand. It buoyed Hughes up. Then we all walked up. It took ten minutes.

We got into the airport lounge area and Hughes brought down the house. He said to them, "I hope you don't mind if I sit on this bar. I've leaned on a few of them over the years." The crowd just howled because these guys all knew him when he was a truck driver and before he quit drinking.

On Election Day 1968 Ed Campbell sent me out to Davenport to vote the first thing in the morning and then drive back to Des Moines. So I did that and came back in the late afternoon. Ed said to go straight to the governor's mansion, which was the old mansion on Grand Avenue. Hughes was there with his wife and daughter. There was a gathering of people. My job at that point was to greet guests and show supporters information. The candidate was behind closed doors.

As the results started coming in around 8:30 or 9 o'clock that night, Hughes was out circulating and came over to me. He said, "Well, Pat, the goddamn ins are out." That was the case. It was a disaster for the Democrats. There were 1.1 million votes cast in the presidential race, and Nixon was beating Humphrey by approximately 148,000 votes. Hughes won the election by 6,415 votes. The Humphrey margin might have been 56 to 44 or 55 to 45 percent or something in that neighborhood. Hughes' margin was more like 50.05 percent. So we won.

The Sam Brown children's brigade was all over the Savery Hotel headquarters, downstairs, upstairs, and on the eighth floor. They stayed all night. I always thought we were going to win. But obviously I was misled. It was touch and go. Around two-thirty or three in the morning we were back over at the Savery Hotel, and I can still remember Campbell gripping my hand and saying, "Thank you, my friend." To me, it was Campbell taking time in a chaotic setting to say, "I do appreciate what you've done."

We won the election in one sense because of the increase in the margin in Ames in Story County and in Iowa City in Johnson County. In those two counties in 1968, we greatly increased Hughes' margin from any previous election. And that had to do with the war in Vietnam and his position with Eugene McCarthy, whom he nominated at the Democratic Convention in 1968. He had established an independence that was widely admired.

Park's take on Hughes was of Hughes' detachment. Hughes was not overly concerned. Of course, Hughes wanted to win the election once he got into it. But he was a guy, who having gone through these wartime experiences, wasn't ever bothered by much. I mean he could get angry, yet he just didn't let stuff bother him. But he did have this ability to inspire.

CHAPTER 2 # EARLY LIFE

ELDER DELUHERY works at Oak Ridge in WW II; wires Alcoa plant in Davenport.

My father, Frank Deluhery, was born in 1910 and died in 1971. He always described himself as "being from up around Dubuque." Dubuque figures very big in our life. My mother, Lucille Donovan Deluhery, came from a farm in Bernard, Iowa, which is in Dubuque County. They met toward the end of the 1930s and were married in 1941 at the cathedral in Dubuque.

George Kennelly, an electrician from Dubuque, brought my father into the electrical trade. The trades matured at the end of the nineteenth century and into the twentieth century. Dad became an electrician in approximately 1934 when he was twenty-four or twenty-five years old. Kennelly got my dad into the International Brotherhood of Electrical Workers (IBEW), and they worked together around Dubuque and on other jobs. My father was always highly complimentary of George and his wife Olive and the role George played in my Dad's life.

But, it was the Depression, and the Depression had this huge impact on my father and mother. The Depression started in 1929 and went all the way through the '30s, with Franklin D. Roosevelt's election in 1932, the New Deal, and the New Deal projects. My father was greatly influenced by the New Deal projects. He worked on various projects with four electricians and a truck, and they slept in the back of the truck while one of them drove to various New Deal projects.

I grew up listening to these stories. For example, one story was about how they'd drive into some little town in their truck on their way to a job, walk into the police station, and explain they were on their way to Colorado or Nevada. They'd ask whether they could sleep all night in the jail. The police officers, if they were in the right place or if the officers were Irish Americans, would let them stay. Then they'd leave the next morning and drive farther west.

When my father and mother were married, World War II was just on the brink of beginning for the American people. They were at a job in Louisville, Kentucky at the time of the bombing of Pearl Harbor. According to my mother, it was a Sunday afternoon, and they were all in a movie theater. The whole crowd heard something had happened. They turned the movie off, and everybody stood up and went out into the streets.

I heard about that not only from my parents, but also from numerous other people about what it was like at the time of the bombing of Pearl Harbor. In American historical terms, the attitude toward the war in Europe and the war in Asia made a 180 degree turn.

My father and mother were in Louisville the day the Kentucky Derby was run, too. My mother always kept a picture from *Life* magazine of one of the horses from the Kentucky Derby. She was expecting a baby, which was me. My godfather, Tom Kennelly, remembers going to the Kentucky Derby and being in the crowd outside the venue. That forged the relationship between the Kennellys and my parents; and later the Kennelly children and the Deluhery children.

George Kennelly, his wife, and their three children were in Louisville with my father working on a job at a gunpowder plant. The next job they went to was in Birmingham, Alabama. I was born in Birmingham, Alabama, on January 31, 1942. George Kennelly's son and daughter became my godparents. Their daughter, Patricia, might have been about thirteen years old. Their son, Tom, was about eleven years old.

I was baptized at a Catholic church in Birmingham. The idea that Tom Kennelly was my godfather and he was only eleven years old meant that he played a huge role in my life. He lives out on the West Coast, and he's still my friend. I've had numerous contacts with him over the years. My folks and the Kennellys were down there for six to eleven months. They worked in Birmingham and Gadsden, Alabama.

There has been a lot of discussion in my lifetime about Birmingham. It wasn't the classic Confederate South. Birmingham had a lot in common with Pittsburgh. It was a manufacturing site. The educational system in the deep South had never recovered from the Civil War. There was segregation so white people and black people were in different schools. The economy in the South never really had taken off after the Civil War the way it had in the North. Both African American and white workers had very poor skills, especially mathematics.

What were they doing in Gadsden, Alabama, and Birmingham, Alabama, working in gunpowder plants? The plants were built in order to produce the munitions needed for the war. They were doing it in the South, which had enormous political power in Washington, D.C. But the population there wasn't prepared to do the work that needed to be done.

I listened to all that while my father was alive. He'd say you couldn't assume the electricians who were working for you in Alabama had the same level of competence as somebody you had worked with in Iowa or Minnesota or Chicago, Illinois. Blacks were on the job site doing common labor, but they weren't electricians. The union and all the building trades didn't allow them in.

So it was an advantage but also a disadvantage that I was born in Birmingham. The advantage was that I grew up in a family that was used to coping with uncertainty and different people. The disadvantage was if you're an Iowa politician born in Birmingham, Alabama, it's not that big of a deal even though I had that in common with other politicians around the country who were born during the war.

There was a U.S. senator from Virginia married to President Lyndon Johnson's daughter whose family had been in Virginia for a long time. But he wasn't born in Virginia because, like me, he was born during World War II. His parents were someplace far away. Sen. John McCain wasn't even born inside the boundaries of the United States of America; he was born in the Canal Zone. Where you were born figures in politics.

After Birmingham, my parents went to Minneapolis, Minnesota for a job. One of my dad's brothers uncovered the Minnesota strand of the Deluhery family that became very big in our life. One was named Keith Deluhery and another Gabe Deluhery. They were all first cousins of my father. Then we went to Chicago, and my mother was about to have another baby, my brother Bob. It was from the late summer of 1943 over into the beginning of 1944. We lived down on the south side; we were near Lake Michigan. We did not have air conditioning, and it was a very hot summer in 1943. My father worked long days and all day Saturday. Maybe they had Sunday morning off. They'd even work Sunday afternoon.

With my mother expecting another baby, my father got another assignment – a plant in Oak Ridge, Tennessee. It was a plant being built and expanded for wartime work. There was no room for wives and children, so he put us on a train to go back to Dubuque. Then he went to Oak Ridge, Tennessee in early 1944.

We had both Donovan and Deluhery relatives in Dubuque. My mother and I were met at the train station by my uncle, Ed Deluhery, who was a Dubuque police officer. My brother, Bob, was born April 23, 1944. My father never saw his second son until World War II was over.

When my Dad was in Tennessee, he didn't know at the time that he was working at an atomic bomb factory. The plant in Oak Ridge figured in the American story in this sense: the New Deal had done the rural electric projects such as the Tennessee Valley Authority. Those New Deal rural electric projects in the 1930s provided a mask for the location of this plant in Tennessee so it would not attract attention. All of this had been going on for about a year. It wasn't wartime work, the reason given for putting the plant in Oak Ridge.

After he was there for about a year, the security forces pulled him into the offices, sat him down, and read off a list of every time he had asked a question that he wasn't authorized to ask or get the answer to.

They had six, eight, or ten items on their list. They said, "You keep asking these questions, and you've been told not to ask questions, but you keep asking them." He said, "I was quite shaken by how thorough they were. So I quit asking questions." He did not know what the purpose of the plant was.

He also said he saw evidence of the capture of scientists in Europe who were brought to Oak Ridge. They were scientists who spoke other languages and were treated like prized race horses, bulls, or something you'd see around a fair. They were fed and taken care of, but there were armed people around who would shoot them if there was some possibility that they could be kidnapped, taken back to Europe, and liberated. There was an enormous amount of security and armed guards around these scientists.

He also saw a married couple, attractive and highly educated American scientists who ate together in a mess hall without much privacy. Dad said they both went through a period when they lost their hair. All their hair fell out, and then they died. He said, "We were all working around this and observed this, trying to figure out what we're doing here."

One of his tasks was to load his dirty clothes in a trunk every couple of weeks and ship them to Dubuque where my mother would do the laundry and ship it back. My mother and father's description of their life in Dubuque and Oak Ridge was that it mirrored the lives of thousands of other Americans. How could you possibly send your clothes to Dubuque to be washed and then have it sent back? That wasn't hard in the wartime economy. Trunks were being sent all over for the very same thing. Laundry facilities and people who would do your laundry were lacking in Oak Ridge.

Whereas, they were using American and European scientists to try to figure out how to set off the atomic bomb. From my father's perspective, he knew there must be some purpose because the plant in Oak Ridge was getting so big. They didn't know the purpose until the bombs were dropped in 1945 on Hiroshima and Nagasaki.

He shared the idea that the war was going to go on for months and months more because the Japanese weren't going to surrender. The Americans thought the Japanese were going to fight to the end. We –

the civilians working on wartime projects and people in uniform – all envisioned a potential end to the war with the Japanese colonizing America. My father didn't want his children and grandchildren growing up subject to the Japanese emperor.

There was a man who ran the maintenance department at Notre Dame who had once lived in Davenport. Ed Lyon said, "You know, at the time of Pearl Harbor, everybody swung around 180 degrees. I and many other people went down to enlist in the military services the next day. Lines formed Monday, Tuesday, and Wednesday for people to get into the military services."

Sometime in the 1940s George Kennelly and his family moved to Minneapolis, Minnesota, and that's where Tom Kennelly and his two sisters grew up. My godfather, Tom Kennelly, went to college in the town where he lived, the College of St. Thomas. It's like St. Ambrose College in Davenport and Loras College in Dubuque, which is owned and run by the diocese. So even in grade school I was aware of Tom Kennelly going to the College of St. Thomas.

Occasionally our family visited Minnesota, and we'd see the Kennellys. We'd stay in a lodge on a summer vacation. Tom had this unbelievable life during the 1950s and 1960s. It had a big impact on me. Number 1, he was in the Marine Corps. Number 2, he was a lawyer. Number 3, he lived in France as a civilian lawyer with the United States government. He sent Christmas cards and postcards to us from France and other places in Europe. His father and mother went over and lived there for ten months.

At the end of the war, my father was able to run a job in Dubuque where my mother was living. We lived out on her family farm in Bernard, Iowa with her mother, her brother, and his two children. So he did the John Deere job in Dubuque in 1945, 1946, and 1947. By then my father was the top electrician on the jobs. He would get jobs like that one partly through his connections in the union.

The contractor on that job was Lightner and Weiser out of Philadelphia. My father's version of the story was that at the end of World War II, there was an immense amount of work to be done and not enough qualified people to do the work. Somebody my father's age – thirty-five in 1945 – with experience was valuable. You would have three or four contractors working at once on the same job site.

The general feeling at the end of the war was that we were going back into the Depression. The military was told not to discharge all the troops at once because if you keep the troops in uniform another three months, six months, nine months or twelve months, at least they can draw pay and send money back home. At a certain point in 1947 or early 1948, there was another job to do, and the IBEW connected my father to a different contractor. They were going to do the Alcoa plant in Davenport. My father was the supervisor of the electricians on the opening of the Alcoa job in Davenport.

During the first three or four months of the job, my mother and her two boys stayed on the farm outside of Dubuque, and my dad went down to Davenport every week and stayed there. He was looking for a place for us to live.

When my father came to Davenport in 1947 to work for a New York contractor, they had a bank account at Davenport Bank. And my father got to know the president there, V.O. Figge. Figge financed my father's early jobs.

The contractor on the Alcoa job was a company named Fischbach & Moore. Harry Fischbach liked my father. My dad was like many other electricians. He was a member of the IBEW, not highly educated, but he had a union card and could run a job. He was terribly excited and happy to be on this job at a site in an onion field along the Mississippi River.

But when they started, it was just a muddy onion field in the spring. Dad brought my mom, my brother, and me down to see the job after a few weeks when we were still in Bernard. She sat in the car and shed tears looking at dad walking in hip boots out into the mud.

When he came back, she said, "Frank, you know there are people who want to hire you at gas and electric utility companies." She said later he was so happy in the hip boots on the job site. He was looking forward to a 2 1/2-year-long contract with Fischbach building this thing and seeing it go from a mud hole to a factory. They finished the first year with almost one mile under roof.

My mother thought, "Well, if you're happy doing that, that's fine, but I feel badly [sic] for you because it looks like it's so dirty and so dangerous." It's a story that endures with me to this day because of the way my father and mother saw the job.

The plant in Davenport was a rolling mill. The plant would take ingots of aluminum that looked like a great big park bench six or eight feet long and four or five feet wide and four or five feet high. The ingots of aluminum were transported to the plant up the Mississippi River and were unloaded there. The ingots were rolled out into long sheets. In the early days the sheets were used for airplane wings. Aluminum was lighter than steel. It was more easily fashioned if you had the right machinery.

Alcoa was headquartered in Pittsburgh, Pennsylvania, a strange place for its headquarters because the aluminum company's basic product came out of Tennessee. Alcoa built the plant in Davenport because it could get a qualified workforce in the Iowa/Illinois Quad Cities that it couldn't get in Tennessee. Alcoa could get workers who could run the very sophisticated machinery.

Fischbach was really a New York contractor. My father would describe him as intelligent. He could make a decision quickly. He had a second guy working for him named Nat Small, company treasurer. They knew how to fight all these battles that you fight in trying to get a job done. They liked my dad because he ran the job efficiently in Scott County, Iowa.

As this first contract was coming to an end, there was a proposal to build the United Nations building in New York City. Fischbach wanted my dad to come out because my dad was a member of the electrical union. My dad always told me he was inclined to take the job. But my mother didn't want to go to New York. Looking back, I'm glad we didn't move to the East Coast. We're very much an Iowa family. In terms of the Greater Midwest, Davenport had much to offer and more so than Dubuque.

So Fischbach offered my dad an alternative: "Why don't you live in Chicago and fly out to New York every week and then come back to Chicago? We would like you there." My mother and father both turned that down.

My dad's version of a meeting with Fischbach and Small was this: "Harry turned just like that and said, 'All right, you set up on your own as an electrical contractor. I'll sell you the equipment, and we'll go forward from there. You'll just be an electrical contractor in Davenport doing the Alcoa job, and we'll find somebody else for New York.'" So Deluhery Electric had a start date of February 1, 1949.

Dad said they made a very good offer, and he took it. They both were business people making a quick decision. He learned from that discussion when people like that make a decision, they don't want to go back and revisit the decision. This is over with; you're out. He was out, but they did facilitate him getting the contract with Alcoa, and the Alcoa job then became a Deluhery Electric job.

When he took over the Alcoa job with Deluhery Electric, he had very good relations with the IBEW. He had been in the union for ten or twelve years. Finding electricians who could do jobs like this was a big challenge, so they were constantly trying to make people into electricians who had wartime work in uniform or not in uniform. He did multiple contracts with Alcoa for the next fifteen years, which kept us in Davenport.

The Alcoa plant had 2 1/2 miles under roof by the time my father sold Deluhery Electric to Ted Deevers, one of his employees, in the mid-1960s. Ted paid my dad off over a three-year period, and then dad was out of it. My father made Deevers change the name from Deluhery Electric to Deevers Electric.

As soon as Deevers paid my dad off and changed the name to Deevers Electric, he went into negotiations with Fischbach to sell it back to them. So then it existed in Davenport for ten or twelve years as Deevers Electric. Their office building was at 819 Swits Street. Deevers had the same deal with Fischbach as my dad had with Ted.

The employees that Fischbach brought in to run Deevers Electric were electricians out of the Chicago area.

Fischbach & Moore eventually became Fischbach Moore & Morrissey. Fischbach had to keep integrating these Irish Catholics into the company, both as partners, supervisors and others, because he was dealing with a 1950s world in which there would be something like thirty-one constituent unions of the AFL-CIO. Every union – electricians, carpenters, plumbers, and the rest – was headed by Irish Catholics. It was a feature of America in the mid-twentieth century that is very meaningful to me because it reverberates across a number of other things. That's the way unions were; that's the way construction was.

My father would go for years to Pittsburgh to negotiate the contracts with Alcoa. In fact, sometimes he would take Deevers, who was the office manager and accountant. Pittsburgh had the infrastructure of the steel industry: attorneys, accountants, trade associations, and all the rest. Even though aluminum competes with steel in a sense, they didn't have those kinds of services in Tennessee. My father would stay in Pittsburgh for a couple of days, maybe three.

When I was growing up, the plant managers and people who were right at the top of the Alcoa plant in Davenport called it the Davenport Works. In the Davenport Works plant, Harry Von Stocker was the key person in the plant responding to the company in Pittsburgh. In the 1950s, we'd take a ride in the Oldsmobile after dinner out east to Locust Street and Jersey Ridge Road, stop at Harry's house, and the two dads would have a short visit while the kids played. Then we'd go buy ice cream.

Co-author's note: On November 1, 2016 Alcoa Inc. spun off its bauxite, alumina, and aluminum operations to a new company called Alcoa Corp. and Alcoa Inc. was renamed Arconic Inc. Arconic Inc. now operates the Davenport Works.

CHAPTER 3
HIGH SCHOOL YEARS

DR. DOOLEY, Kennellys, trip to D.C. and New York portend adventurous path.

When I was a freshman and sophomore at St. Ambrose Academy, we had students who had come from behind the Iron Curtain. They were from places such as Hungary and Poland. They were refugees who had been connected to small rebellions against Soviet domination and then spirited out of the country by missionary priests. How did they land in Davenport? There were all these networks inside the Catholic Church to facilitate that kind of a transfer.

In Davenport, I could go to the building and right to the room where we had two freedom fighters from Hungary. They were a little older than me; they might have been seventeen or eighteen my freshman year. We had a student come in during the first year at Assumption High School named Stash Melizsewski. Stash was my brother's age, two years behind me. He had an older brother named Leonard and a younger brother named Cozzy.

Years later, Stash's mother supported me in the 1978 campaign. They spoke very broken English. Jim Leach was able to get Stash recruited to go to Princeton University where he played football. He and my brother were heavyweight wrestlers.

A quick note about Jim Leach, a friend who went on to be a congressman for several decades. Jim and I are the same age, and we met almost immediately upon our graduation from high school in 1960. He'd gone to Davenport High – we played football against each other in the fall of 1959.

In my junior year at newly-opened Assumption High School, the boys' division was on one side, and the girls' division was on the other side of the school. But the journalism class was mixed. I was in the journalism class with several other boys and girls. The teacher was a very imaginative, energetic teacher named Father William Wiebler who advised the school newspaper. They had a contest to name it. I submitted the name the *Knight Beacon* and won the contest.

By the spring of my junior year, the journalism students were more or less running the school newspaper. The seniors were so eager to get out of there, they no longer wanted to do any work. So I became the editor of the *Knight Beacon* in my senior year and that had a huge impact on my life. I learned how to write the stories and get the paper out.

Like the previous year, I experienced "senioritis." By January and February 1960, I didn't want to do all these jobs anymore; I was turning things down. But the experience was very good for me. I have talked to journalists frequently about trying to find the story in something that's very complex. I tried to teach my students at St. Ambrose the concept of audience.

That is, what is the audience you're preparing for? What is their level of understanding and how can you find a lead? How can you even find the first word of the story that will draw them into it? That's constantly the challenge in politics. It was the challenge in the Hughes campaign of 1968, the Fulton campaign of 1970, the Franzenburg campaign of 1972, the Culver campaign of 1974, and in my own campaigns as well.

Journalism was always a possible option for me. But there were other options as well that I never was able to take advantage of. So I didn't go into journalism or banking although I was recruited to go into banking and financial services in Davenport, New York City, and Washington, D.C. There always were so many options that I had to stick to one.

The guy who gave me advice on that was John Culver. Culver had been a high school star athlete, finishing high school in about 1950. He came from a family that was well connected in Cedar Rapids. His father and grandfather were graduates of Harvard University. When Culver finished high school in 1950 and went to Harvard, he fell in immediately. His best friend for four years was Ted Kennedy. He was Kennedy's first administrative assistant when Ted was elected a U.S. senator in 1962, in the seat held earlier by his brother.

In high school we were members of a group called Young Christian Students. We met once a month and discussed some religious topic. It was always a social justice message. I was reminded of these discussions later in life when watching movies such as *On the Waterfront* with Marlon Brando. A priest in that movie had a social justice message.

My dad encouraged me to go to the University of Notre Dame. I couldn't go there in the fall of 1959 for a big football game my dad had organized, however. The priest at Davenport Assumption High School, Father Art Perry, had played football at Notre Dame ten or twelve years earlier. He took a carload of boys from high school to Notre Dame for this football game. I was invited, of course, because my dad had put the whole trip together as an indirect way to say, "Maybe you want to go to Notre Dame." But I couldn't go because I'd broken my foot – in a football game!

Father Perry showed up at our house one night in early December and said, "Pat, what do you think about applying to Notre Dame?" I said, "Fine." That did sound good to me, though I hadn't really given it a lot of thought. So we filled out the application, and I sent it in. My acceptance letter from Notre Dame arrived on March 17, 1960 – St. Patrick's Day. There was a party that night at a fellow's house on Locust Street.

We decided to visit Notre Dame in the summer of 1960. I'd also been invited to be part of the Honors Program. We spent a couple of days there. Five or six priests from the Davenport Diocese were there taking summer classes, so we had dinner with them. I remember the priests said to Dad as dinner was finishing, "Could Pat and Bob go with us? We're going to an Alfred Hitchcock movie. We'll get them back to the hotel when the movie is over." That night we saw *Psycho*, one of Hitchcock's best.

Father Marvin Mottet, who came from a family near Ottumwa, had a big role in my life. I had him two or three times as a high school teacher. He taught the religion class in my senior year. He was a very good teacher. He had us read six books and do six book reports in the fall and read six more in the spring. The books included George Orwell's *1984* and *Animal Farm. The Last Hurrah* by Edwin O'Connor was another one.

Father Mottet had a really strong social justice commitment. Apart from reading those iconic novels, we also dealt with the social justice message of the American Catholic Church, particularly in the Davenport Diocese. Father Mottet had a very good friend named Charles Toney, a black Catholic. It was a strand of American life that cut across these other strands: Davenport was a river town and was industrialized so it had a big labor union presence.

Around the fall of 1959, when I was still in high school, Father Mottet and another priest took two carloads of boys from Davenport Assumption High School to Chicago for the day. After we drove over to Chicago, we were ushered into this big banquet hall where we were allowed to sit above the ground floor. The banquet hall might have had five hundred tables of ten people each. A couple thousand more people were up in the balcony around the outside of the banquet hall.

The speaker was named Dr. Tom Dooley, a medical doctor who had connections with the drug industry. He would get the drug industry to donate the drugs to his workplace in Southeast Asia. It was called French Indochina in those days. It was Vietnam, Cambodia, Laos, and other places.

When the French were driven out of Southeast Asia, the Americans under President Eisenhower moved in. There were all these unlikely connections. The Catholic Church in Southeast Asia was not a majority, but it did have a significant presence.

Dr. Dooley became something of a hero to some Southeast Asians and North Americans because his work improved health care for people in Southeast Asia. A Notre Dame graduate, Dr. Dooley was very charismatic. His speech was about his work, and it opened up a wider world for high school students.

The priests said at the end of the luncheon, "Now we've arranged to go to a Maryknoll house and introduce you guys to these Maryknoll missionaries." The missionaries might have been at the luncheon, as well.

We met Father Laurence Murphy at the Maryknoll house. Maryknoll is a Catholic order of missionary priests with a place outside of New York City and another place in the Chicago area. (Father Murphy would marry Mardi and me in Washington, D.C. in 1973.) We visited with Father Murphy about Southeast Asia and Dooley's work abroad. I don't know why the priests in Davenport lined that up. They were introducing us to a wider world. They were very good teachers.

Father Bill Dawson also was one of my teachers in Davenport. He and I spent four years together at Notre Dame because he was a graduate student studying for a doctorate. He finished his doctorate about the same time I finished my undergraduate degree. Later on when I came back to Davenport, he was one of the people on the staff at St. Ambrose College and was one of the people who gave me a good recommendation to leadership there.

In 1959, I was a senior at Davenport Assumption High School, George and Olive Kennelly came through Davenport on their way back from France headed to the West Coast, and they stayed at our house for four or five days. During the visit we were having one of our high school dances. I was going to the dance; I was able to drive. I had another friend, so we went to the dance with our dates in the Gold Room at Hotel Blackhawk. It was probably the homecoming dance in the fall.

After I was out of the house, my father said, "Well, George and Olive, would you like to go down to the dance?" Well, of course, they'd like to go down to the dance. They were energetic, lively people. So my mother and Olive had to figure out what they were going to wear, which took a while. They got down to the dance at maybe 9 or 9:15 p.m. Then my father organized a table where the four of them sat, and the priests at Assumption High School and other parents who were chaperones gathered at the table.

My father bought a bottle or two of champagne on ice, and George Kennelly sat at the front of the table and regaled them with stories of what it's like to live in France when you can't speak French, including being hospitalized. Other students would say to me, "You know, your dad is over at that other table." I'd say, "Yeah, I know he is. I know just what's going on. It's great. It's fine." In other words, I knew what they were doing, and I didn't mind. Of course, the high school faculty and the parents of some of the other students who knew my parents enjoyed all of that immensely. It was a whole evening of stories.

I was a senior in high school in the spring of 1960 during Lent. Mother and I would walk over to Mass at 6:30 a.m. at St. Paul the Apostle Church close to our house. I remember my mother saying very distinctly, "Well, that Sen. John F. Kennedy won the Wisconsin primary last night, and maybe he's got a chance to run for president this fall."

I had a priest teacher in high school named Father John Boyle. He had come to St. Ambrose Academy my sophomore year. I remember him teaching modern European history. He was very well educated. He had grown up in Iowa City and gone into the Catholic Church priesthood, but he was sent to Rome, Italy for four years of theological training. He visited our house occasionally. My parents encouraged me to be in this scholar's classes.

When I finished high school in 1960, I had already traveled a couple of times to Chicago with high school friends John and Tom McDonnell and later with my brother, Bob.

In the summer of 1960 Father Boyle drove me and my brother to Washington, D.C. Father Boyle had six weeks of classwork to take at Catholic University of America in Washington, D.C. My brother and I had an aunt named Catherine Augusta Donovan, a single woman who lived at McLean Gardens in Washington, D.C. She offered to keep us for four or six weeks in the summer of 1960.

We'd go to the House of Representatives at the U.S. Capitol every day and go to the office of U.S. Rep. Fred Schwengel, an Iowa congressman who represented Davenport. His home was along West Locust Street not far from the fairgrounds and not far from West High in Davenport. Later I served in the Iowa Senate with his brother, Frosty Schwengels of southeast Iowa, who spelled his last name slightly differently.

We went to several House and Senate hearings on various subjects. One was related to corruption in the boxing industry. The name of the witness was Jake LaMotta. I had seen him box Sugar Ray Robinson on television in the 1950s. LaMotta no longer was an active boxer by 1960, but he talked about corruption in the boxing industry. LaMotta described what he had to deal with. He was kind of an angry, argumentative witness. It was quite memorable. LaMotta was the subject of a very famous movie called *Raging Bull* a decade or so later.

We also went canoeing on the Potomac River with one of the young men we met at McLean Gardens. We had a wonderful summer doing all of that. We owe all of that in a sense to Father Boyle driving us to Washington, D.C. and Aunt Augusta keeping us.

At the end of the three weeks or so, we took the train up to New York City. Neither one of us had ever been in New York City; I still don't remember how we arranged this. We got a room in the Plaza Hotel, the iconic hotel at the corner of Central Park, 59th Street and Fifth Avenue. We were there for three, four, or five days. We visited St. Patrick's Cathedral and the United Nations. We were at Times Square and the Empire State Building.

When we were at the top of the Empire State Building, we made a long distance phone call back to Davenport to talk to my dad and mom. It was a very important summer trip for me because a few weeks later when I arrived at the University of Notre Dame as a freshman, it had an impact on my relations with all the other freshmen I met at Notre Dame.

Not too long after George and Olive Kennelly came through Davenport, maybe the summer of 1960, Tom Kennelly came through. He was driving his own car, and he had a dog. The dog was named Jacques. He described all the stuff he had been doing in Europe the last three or four years as a Marine Corps officer and later as a civilian attorney working for the U.S. government. One of our neighbors could speak French. She spoke to the dog in French and the dog responded. The dog was terribly happy to hear someone speak in French!

So Tom did all of these things in short order in the summer of 1960 and all the way through the next three or four years. He went to the West Coast and got a job with a man named Cecil Pool, who was an African American judge. Tom was a graduate of the University of Santa Clara College of Law, which is a Jesuit college and law school. We had visited the Kennellys in California in approximately 1955, so I had seen Tom when he was a law student about ready to take the bar exam.

These kinds of influences laid a path for my future. My father and mother encouraged me to be adventuresome, deal with the outside world, take on the unexpected, and turn that into stories you could tell for months and years. The Kennellys and their son coming back from France set me on that course.

Later, when people asked how I got the idea of going to school in London, I knew the two people responsible for that, besides my parents, were Tom Kennelly and Father John Boyle. They did not suggest the London School of Economics, but the example of their lives, plus my father's vivid stories of life on the road in the 1930s, informed my choices.

CHAPTER 4

NOTRE DAME DAYS

UNDERGRADUATE experience includes Honors Program, Kennedy victory, Peru.

In those days the school year at Notre Dame started on approximately September 20. A lot of other colleges started a week or ten days before that. I found out when I got there I had been selected for the Honors Program. I remembered I'd been sent a note that summer asking if I was willing to sign up for the Honors Program and I'd said yes. I got my schedule; one of my first teachers was Frank O'Malley. I was so naïve.

We had four guys in the Honors class who had gone to Georgetown Prep in Washington, D.C. One of them, Clark McGranery, was the son of an attorney general of the United States during the last year of President Harry Truman's administration. Clark had an older brother who was a junior at Notre Dame.

There was another guy, Walt Duncan, who had gone to Portsmouth Priory in Portsmouth, New Hampshire. He was from Oklahoma, and his father and grandfather had gone to Notre Dame. There were three or four more guys in the Honors class, one of whom is a friend of mine to this day. His name is Vince DeCoursey.

One of them was named Frank McConnell. He was a very brilliant, slender, small little fellow ... very cocky and full of himself. But he was a very good guy to have in the class because like me, he was not intimidated by the grandeur of everybody else's credentials. And I wasn't. I just kind of took it for granted that I was in this class.

It turned out that Frank O'Malley was practically an iconic figure at Notre Dame. He'd been around campus since he'd graduated thirty years or so earlier. O'Malley had had this student named Edwin O'Connor in class ten or twelve years earlier. O'Connor came and spent a week at Notre Dame every year. O'Connor was the author of a novel called *The Last Hurrah* that had been a runaway best seller. We had read *The Last Hurrah* at our house. My mother and I had read the book *The Last Hurrah* when I was in high school, and I loved the novel. O'Connor was writing another book called *The Edge of Sadness* about an alcoholic priest in recovery.

So O'Connor joined our class for two or three sessions that week. I'd have visits with him along with other people in O'Malley's group. That played a role in my life. There weren't a lot of girls available so we didn't date a lot. We were introduced to this overseas and national milieu. I had little appreciation of how iconic it was. You could go to a football game out of state, such as Pittsburgh in Pittsburgh, or Navy in Baltimore once a season. There would be six, seven, or eight busloads of Notre Dame students go to a game like that. Then after the game, we'd be bussed up to New York City and we'd stay all night in a hotel.

In another sense I was in way over my head academically. That is, I was in very deep water academically in the Honors Program because most of the other twenty-two or so people in the class had been to prep schools, which were almost like college. In fact, that was the joke we made about the guy who went to Portsmouth Priory. He did college when he was in high school and he did high school when he was in college. Why was that? He and others had gone to these high schools that were so disciplined, focused on writing skills, mathematics, and the cutting edge of whatever was going on.

My high school in Davenport had given me a very good education because it encouraged curiosity, expression of your ideas, and an enormous amount of knowledge about social justice issues. So I knew all about labor unions and the fights of 1930s, 1940s, and 1950s over equal rights for working people and minorities, both African American and Hispanic – more so than the East Coast guys who went to Georgetown Prep. On the other hand, they knew how to hit the ball out of the park when they were given writing assignments, whereas I was floundering in a lot of the classes.

O'Malley got a big kick out of me and encouraged me in the class. I was not afraid of him; therefore, I'd speak up and bounce things back and forth with him. I remember very clearly that on the first day of class, he said, "I'd like some of you to introduce yourselves." He'd look at somebody and call on him and say, "You're Dick Marks from some prep school in New York City." And he'd ask, "Are you on scholarship?" And Dick would say he'd been awarded this distinguished scholarship that either Notre Dame had given him or he'd won in New York. And then O'Malley asked a second guy, probably Frank McConnell from Louisville, Kentucky, "Have you been awarded a fellowship or scholarship?" Frank piped up with whatever he'd been awarded.

So I smiled at O'Malley and he said, "You're Pat Deluhery from Davenport, Iowa. Are you on a fellowship or scholarship?" I said, "I'm on the Frank B. Deluhery Memorial Fellowship." And O'Malley liked it. He smiled and laughed. Then he said, "You're kidding." And I nodded yes. And he said, "Not bad." Some of the other people in class were shocked that I would be so forward with this distinguished teacher.

Matthew Fitzsimmons was another teacher I had at Notre Dame. He taught the freshman Honors history class. I crossed paths with Fitzsimmons a few times later in life. In 1966-67 when I was living in London, I bought tickets to an opera in downtown London. As I went in, there was Fitzsimmons and his wife with a couple of others. I said hello to him right away. So we went to the opera together.

About this time, the primary for governor of Iowa was going on. The Democratic side had two candidates who were widely known: Edward McManus from southeast Iowa and (Harold) Hughes. McManus defeated Hughes in the 1960 Democratic primary for governor. McManus was a tall, black-haired Irish man and a very good speaker. He was very well educated with a bachelor's degree and a law degree. He was widely known up and down the east side of the state. But

Hughes didn't leave office; he was Iowa Commerce commissioner elected in 1958 with Herschel Loveless. So Hughes was able to serve two more years. McManus lost the gubernatorial race to Republican Norman Erbe, but he was appointed a federal judge in Iowa by President Kennedy in 1961.

As September became October then November 1960, we were all terribly excited about the candidacy of John F. Kennedy. His victory in November was a signal achievement for what we regarded as the Irish and Catholic community of North America. We were so excited, and it meant so much to us to see John F. Kennedy become president. That whole saga of 1961, '62, and '63 played a big role in my life, following politics and the Kennedy administration.

There's plenty that's been written about Kennedy. I had seen Kennedy that summer of 1960 as the guest of congressman Schwengel. He escorted us over to the Senate one day and arranged for us to go up into the vice president's box. The vice president's box is directly opposite the presiding officer of the Senate and it faces down over the Senate floor.

My brother and I sat in the front row and we heard John F. Kennedy give a speech about the student loan program. He was opposed to loyalty oaths that had been imposed on the students who got loans in the federal program. Kennedy was quoting several people saying this is ridiculous. It's adding some kind of a bureaucratic guilt trip to students who win scholarships and loans from the federal government.

Among others, he quoted Notre Dame president Theodore Hesburgh. When Kennedy finished the speech, he walked up to the presiding officer's box, which was directly opposite to us from where we were sitting, laid some papers down, and then turned around and headed back to where he sat.

My brother and I were smiling at him. We didn't wave our hands, but he looked up. He would know that was the vice president's box and that if he won the nomination for president in the next month or so, he'd be running against Vice President Richard Nixon. Nonetheless, he could see friendly faces so he smiled back and nodded.

When you had Kennedy's attention, you had his undivided attention. He paid close attention to you for thirty or sixty seconds. He looked you in the eye and heard what you said and was ready to ask a question if it occurred to him.

Of course, we also saw Lyndon Johnson, who was a fabulous parliamentarian, public policy guy. Johnson and his people were in charge of everything the Senate did. He outranked Kennedy in terms of his position in the U.S. Senate. They were rivals for the nomination and, of course, Johnson became his vice presidential candidate and vice president and succeeded Kennedy on Kennedy's death in 1963. We were in the vice presidential box several times, so Johnson saw us. He noticed everything.

Johnson had this big personality. I met Johnson after he left the presidency at an event in Washington, D.C. We were all at a big dinner to raise money for the U.S. Senate on the Democratic side. Johnson came down this long corridor to get to the event. I was going to the event representing Harold Hughes. I stopped. As he came swooping by me, he stopped with his wife. I put my hand out and said, "I'm Pat Deluhery. I work for Harold Hughes." In a big voice, he said, "I'm so happy to meet you. Say hello to my wife, Bird." She smiled. And off they went.

I've bought and read books by Robert Caro about Johnson. Johnson was unbelievably productive and ambitious. Hughes liked Johnson, although he was critical of Johnson over the war in Vietnam. That was all before I went to work for Hughes. Hughes had supported Johnson in the early 1960s and not Kennedy. There's a cartoon about Johnson and Hughes that ran in the *Des Moines Register* about how well Hughes had done in the 1964 landslide.

———

I had a friend, Dick Wolfe, whose parents lived on a farm near Lost Nation, Iowa. The farm is about forty miles north of Davenport. Wolfe had a couple of brothers living in Davenport. One was an enormously successful businessman in the beverage industry; the other was a teacher at St. Ambrose College. Dick's parents arranged for him to come down and do his last two years of high school at Davenport Assumption High School and live with one of his brothers. I visited Lost Nation and their farm that fall after the election of 1960.

Dick Wolfe's mother said to me about the presidential election, "Well, Pat, it was Ezra Taft Benson against the Pope, and the Pope lost." The meaning of that was then, as in the Nixon administration in 1972 and as in today's Trump administration, farmers often feel they're getting the short end of the stick. Often they don't know about these openings abroad or other things. They're the last to learn about it even if the secretary of agriculture theoretically is working on their behalf.

The secretary of agriculture under President Dwight Eisenhower was Ezra Taft Benson. He was wildly unpopular among Iowa farmers. On the other hand, John F. Kennedy being Catholic wasn't going to carry Iowa and he lost big-time in Iowa. Lost Nation was a place where people went to one church or another church and then they went to one bar or another bar, and they didn't go to the same places when they were in church or at a bar. Or at least that's my impression. When we were seniors in high school, I appointed Dick Wolfe sports editor of the *Knight Beacon*. We were classmates at Notre Dame. Dick has become a very successful writer of books about sports personalities and their fans.

In the spring of 1961 there was a little notice on campus that there was going to be a priest describing the Kennedy initiative called the Peace Corps. I went to the meeting in the basement meeting room of one of the residence halls. The speaker was Father Laurence Murphy. I didn't realize at the time I had met him earlier until I saw him. There weren't that many students at the meeting. I went up and talked to him at the end of the meeting; it turned out he was a candidate for a doctorate at Notre Dame. Many other religious orders had priests on campus; the priests would teach some classes and probably do some work in Chicago at one of their seminaries. I got to know Father Murphy that day.

Before long that spring, he came over to my residence hall and asked the rector of the residence hall, "Could Pat Deluhery join me? I have a speaking invitation in Pennsylvania, and maybe we'll drive over to Pennsylvania and be gone for a couple of days." The rector said, "Fine." And that's what we did. So I left with Father Murphy from South Bend to go to Pennsylvania that spring of 1961. We went to a place called Gannon College in Erie, Pennsylvania.

A few things happened as a result of connecting with Father Murphy. First, we organized a group on campus in the spring of 1961 to reach out to the Mexican migrant workers who were working in the South Bend, Indiana area. They were having a Sunday afternoon celebration at the end of the migrant season. The women in the party prepared a Mexican-style meal.

Then the Notre Dame students and the men, women, and children shared a meal together. We were trying to reach out to them and be friendly. It loomed quite large in this sense: during my four years at Notre Dame, that was the beginning of a group called the Council for the International Lay Apostolate. Father Murphy was very much behind that. He was a Maryknoll missionary, but he had global experience since World War II in both Asia and South America.

Second, Father Theodore Hesburgh, who was the president of Notre Dame, wanted to have a more globally-interested student body, so he encouraged it. They built a building on the Notre Dame campus near the library that was the headquarters for the lay apostolate movement. They tore down that building and built a bigger building, which is still the headquarters of the lay apostolate.

Third, I was invited to speak at the dedication of the building twenty years after I graduated, probably through contacts with Father Murphy and President Father Hesburgh.

One of the students who went on one of these summer trips was named Ed Malloy from Washington, D.C. He was a year ahead of me and later became president of Notre Dame. They called him Monk; he was a basketball player.

These events originated from a different view of the Catholic Church in North America and its interest in global affairs. It was after World War II and during the Kennedy administration. There was an enormous amount of idealism attached to all of that. I was invited back in the last five or six years to go to Notre Dame for a description of the beginning of the Council for the International Lay Apostolate. It's now part of the Notre Dame global initiative that's still centered in that building.

We had a speaker named William F. Buckley on campus in 1961 during my freshman year at Notre Dame. He was the main force behind a conservative publication called *The National Review*. I remember thinking I have to ask a question; I'm not going to just sit here. Most of the students who were there probably were more in agreement with Buckley than me. I asked him a question, and he volleyed it back at me in a way that was kind of humorous. I said Number 1, Number 2, Number 3, and what do you make of that? And he volleyed it back, Number 4, I don't think you're correct. That got a laugh out of the crowd, but I didn't mind. I'd overcome any anxiety I had had about trying to ask a question. That kind of experience was available all four years at Notre Dame.

By the summer of 1962 we launched our first international project, and I went on it. Eight students from Notre Dame went to a place in Lima, Peru for eight weeks. It stemmed from Father Murphy's Maryknoll background; he was used to stuff going on around the world. It also reflected Father Hesburgh's interest that Notre Dame students be more interested in the world and those kinds of issues. We still wanted to have good football teams, but by then, Hesburgh had been president of Notre Dame for about ten years, and he was trying to change the direction of Notre Dame in some sense. Father Murphy very much agreed with that.

My father very much supported the trip to Peru. None of us in our family had ever gone outside the United States. My father and mother's connection to a different country would be Ireland – my father's grandfather who was an immigrant in the late 1840s. That grandfather was deceased before my father was born. So we were not traveled in that sense. My father also spent World War II doing defense work – not going overseas for military service. So we did not have that kind of international exposure in our family. On the other hand, a lot of things changed for me when I was admitted to the University of Notre Dame.

I learned some Spanish in 1962. It was a very successful summer for me. We visited a Catholic parish in what would be regarded today as a new town. The new town was on the edge of Lima, Peru and it was called Ciudad de Dios, or City of God. There was a Catholic Church there staffed by Maryknoll missionaries. We worked on a variety of projects. I didn't realize how prestigious the University of Notre Dame was to the leadership of the Catholic Church and the government in Lima. On occasion we were invited to the American Embassy with staff people, big figures, and other people swirling around them. We met the Cardinal archbishop of Peru, the president of Peru, and the Papal Nuncio who was like the papal ambassador from the Vatican to Peru.

These gatherings had something in common with those two years earlier when I was in Washington, D.C. and with a lot of social gatherings I attended at Notre Dame around big events such as a football game or a guest speaker from some prestigious place. Whatever the big event was, there frequently would be social mixers afterwards or the next day. All of that was a big-eye opener for me – American involvement in an international world.

Later I learned there was a student one year older than me named Tony Bill. I saw him perform several times in shows and plays – mainly on the St. Mary's campus. In my junior year he graduated from college. He had gone in to see the dean of the College of Arts and Letters in the spring of 1963. The dean made one call and arranged for Bill to have an audition in Hollywood. Bill was in the movie *Come Blow Your Horn* with Frank Sinatra just like that. The movie came out while I was a senior in college.

I saw Bill interviewed in the last few days. It was an old interview that ran on the *Showtime* network about pornography in the movies. Bill had a long career in Hollywood as an actor and producer. He was the producer of the movie *The Sting* starring Paul Newman and Robert Redford. When I was in London, Bill performed in a London production about the assassination of President Kennedy with

Bill playing Lee Harvey Oswald. He was immensely talented and connected. For years, he was known for having a restaurant up the coast from Hollywood.

It gave me the idea in the fall of 1963 that if I went to talk to Father Charles Sheedy, the dean of the College of Arts and Letters, he might open doors for me. I told him, "I think I might like to go to the London School of Economics when I graduate. I know I've got faculty members here laying the groundwork for me to pursue a doctorate in English literature, but what I feel like doing is going to London." I remember Father Sheedy saying, "Well, I think people ought to do what they feel like doing."

So Sheedy arranged for me to get the mailings from the LSE.

Later, I visited a second person on campus named George Shuster. He was a Notre Dame graduate who was the age of my father. In 1963-64, Shuster was on campus as an assistant to Father Hesburgh. So I arranged a visit with Shuster and told him what I was thinking about doing. I said, "Maybe I'd like to go to the London School of Economics." I remember Shuster saying, "Well, people ought to do what they feel like doing."

That visit with Shuster is what allowed me to be admitted to the London School of Economics. I never knew who wrote the letters. But Shuster was a person who moved comfortably across those European capitals. I never got a straight story from Shuster or anybody else regarding what they might have done about that. But either Shuster or Father Hesburgh signed a letter to the London School of Economics saying that if Pat Deluhery wants to come and you can admit him, give him a fair shot.

In the late 1930s or early 1940s, George Shuster was president of Hunter College in New York City. He had assisted in the post-World War II reconstruction of Germany. In other words, he had gone to Germany under the sponsorship of the Defense Department or State Department immediately at the close of World War II. He might have been there as a civilian before World War II ended. Who knows? At that time, the predecessor to the Central Intelligence Agency was the OSS, the Office of Strategic Services. Shuster might have been associated with that.

The whole 1945, '46, '47 history of central Europe, the Marshall Plan, the airlift of supplies to Berlin when Berlin was inside East Germany, the unraveling of the World War II coalition of the United States of America, Britain, Russia, and the Free French – all of that was part of Shuster's portfolio of things he had done as a younger man.

Shuster, Hesburgh, and others were trying to bring Notre Dame forward. Previously, Notre Dame had been this school in the Midwest that drew students mainly from the Midwest and East Coast and partly from the West Coast. Hesburgh was making it a nationwide university with students from all fifty states including a huge presence in California.

Hesburgh opened an office in California with one person who raised money, one who watched for football players, one who connected with the academic world in California, and one who ran the office. They probably had a huge presence with the Catholic Church in California. They'd also be interested in the Hispanic community in California.

So I applied to the London School of Economics and was admitted on the condition that I graduate with honors from the University of Notre Dame. My academic credentials at Notre Dame had improved solidly over the four years I was there.

In 1960 Republican Jack Miller was elected to the U.S. Senate and another Republican, Bourke Hickenlooper, was serving in the Senate. On the 1962 ballot, Democrat E.B. Smith ran against Hickenlooper. There was a lot of enthusiasm for Smith; I believe he'd taught at Iowa State University in Ames. But Hickenlooper won, and Smith didn't. Hughes once said to me, "Something happened in 1962 that caused E.B. Smith to lose." It was the Cuban missile crisis. President Kennedy had invited a bunch of senators to come back to Washington in the middle of that crisis to consult with the president. And one of them was Hickenlooper who was widely respected.

In 1963 Hughes was confronting a negative Legislature and the Baker vs. Carr decision on properly apportioning the U.S. House of Representatives, Iowa Senate, Iowa House of Representatives, and state legislatures around the nation. When Hughes ran for reelection in 1964, the political map was chaotic. Nobody knew what was going on. They were recruiting candidates who never had been to the Capitol or didn't know very much about politics and government.

One guy was elected in Sioux City and was told, "Well, you're going to be a representative." His answer was, "Yeah, and I've never been to Washington." He didn't know he was going to Des Moines! Hughes started his second term in 1965 with huge majorities in both houses of the Legislature and in a modernized Iowa.

President Kennedy's assassination on November 22, 1963 was a major event in the life of many Americans. I remember going over to the chapel at Notre Dame for the 4 o'clock mass that day. George Shuster was there. His job at Notre Dame was being an assistant to the president.

That weekend, Father Laurence Murphy was driving to the East Coast. So a bunch of us jumped in the car to drive to the East Coast with Father Murphy. There were people in Washington, D.C. who were friends of mine. They'd finished Notre Dame and had gone to Georgetown University. One of them was named Billy Moran. Later, he wound up in Chicago. Father Murphy got me as far as Philadelphia, and then I took the train down to Washington on the Sunday night after Kennedy's assassination and stayed all night with Moran.

I was on the streets for the John F. Kennedy funeral and funeral procession on Monday, Tuesday, and Wednesday. I was with the crowd when Sen. Ted Kennedy, Attorney General Bobby Kennedy, the widow Jacqueline Kennedy, and the family walked by. Behind them were these people from around the world: Haile Selassie and Charles de Gaulle, a small dark man from North Africa next to this tall French man who had led the Free French forces from outside France during World War II.

For me, those kinds of experiences were very real and meaningful.

No, I did not take pictures. I went to the Kennedy grave at Arlington National Cemetery the next day. I had dinner that night with St. Mary's College graduate Arline Hagen and Tom Kennelly. I said, "Maybe I'll go to London."

In 1963 and '64 Park Rinard was at the League of Iowa Municipalities and writing the remarks as a behind-the-scenes adviser. Park's role in the campaign and in guiding the policy positions that came out of the governor's mouth and his office was not widely known by the top journalists. A person with a journalism background named Dwight Jensen became the chief of staff for Hughes.

Over the next six years, Hughes added several other people with various backgrounds. One of the first was Bill Hedlund, who lives in Des Moines and is still a friend of mine. It was Hedlund's job to drive at night to Park's house to pick up written words and drive to the office. Then the words would be reproduced in the office under Jensen's supervision. The press gave Dwight Jensen credit for how terrifically good Harold Hughes' speeches were and what amazing timing Jensen had on releasing press releases and hitting the ball just when it needed to be hit.

So Jensen and the office staff always got a lot of praise. It was not out of line because Jensen was very capable – he had a journalistic background and he learned how to run that office. And they were back on the ballot in 1964.

Everything else at the state Capitol was held by Republicans in 1963. A cartoon in the *Des Moines Register* showed Hughes as a great big donkey with six Republican elephants around him kind of looking uneasily at Hughes. His wife, Eva, told me the Republican establishment in Des Moines and Iowa made it very tough on them when they moved into the governor's mansion. A lot of the portable fixtures such as lamps and household appliances disappeared.

The wedding of Tom and Susie Kennelly in the spring of 1964 was another major event for me. By then, my godfather Tom Kennelly had been living in Washington, D.C. for approximately three years. He had moved to Washington from San Francisco to work for Attorney General Bobby Kennedy in the new Kennedy administration. Tom set up Bobby Kennedy's initiative called strike forces. The strike forces were a version of law enforcement that focused on the various crimes committed in a particular region.

The target of the strike force was the Magaddino family of Buffalo, New York. You would get law enforcement at the local, state, and federal level together. You would get very strict secrecy and no tipping off the targets. You'd look at all the things associated with organized crime – alcohol, gambling, prostitution, small crimes, theft, and murder. But you had to have very strict control of who was working on the strike force from all the various law enforcement agencies.

Tom would describe all of that to our family. It was impressive in one sense, but it also was tipping over the apple cart of the American law enforcement community. Law enforcement is typically a local government function. Security of information is not something you can count on when you're dealing with multiple officers and different agencies. It was a very demanding and difficult task to gather a team and then keep the information close at hand. But that was Tom Kennelly's job for Bobby Kennedy in 1961, 1962, and 1963.

I was a student at Notre Dame during those years. Tom Kennelly occasionally was in the Chicago area on behalf of the Justice Department. He came to a football game in the fall of 1963 at Notre Dame. I saw him a fair amount of time. At a very early age, I was introduced to what was going on in Washington, D.C.

When Tom was getting married around Easter 1964, our family went to Washington, D.C. for the wedding. My brother, Bob, could not go; he was a student at St. Norbert College in DePere, Wisconsin. The wedding had a huge effect on me. I didn't know yet whether I was going to be admitted to the London School of Economics, but we had a grand time in Washington for three or four days. It introduced me to Catholic University of America where our two daughters graduated. Tom's wife, who was from the Omaha, Nebraska area, had graduated from Catholic University.

CHAPTER 5

OFF TO LONDON

OAKESHOTT, the Six, Malcolm X, Beatles, Dylan are part of the scene in '60s.

In June 1964 I learned right away I was graduating with honors and that I was admitted to the London School of Economics. At the time, we hardly knew the name Vietnam. We thought of Southeast Asia as the place where Dr. Tom Dooley had been doing a lot of work with missionaries. There was a Catholic community in Southeast Asia.

The American government in partitioning Vietnam into North and South Vietnam in the 1950s was carrying out an understanding of worldwide communism that resulted from the very bitter breakup of the allies at the end of World War II. Germany was divided into West and East Germany. The Soviet Union under Stalin's leadership had occupied Eastern Europe.

Winston Churchill had used a phrase in this country: "The Iron Curtain has descended on Europe." So Churchill's Iron Curtain was very real in our lives in the 1950s and early 1960s.

There's been a long debate over whether President Kennedy would have continued to fight the war in Vietnam. His brother, Bobby, became a very vocal critic by 1968. President Johnson and the people around him were all saying we had to stop communism in Vietnam or it would come to Hawaii and the West Coast.

But for many people in my generation, that was not something we accepted very easily. In fact, many of us did not accept it at all. It seemed to many of us in the summer of 1964 that it was a war on the side of the colonial powers trying to hold onto the countries they had colonized. Whatever the North Vietnam communists were like, what did we have to gain by fighting over there?

One of my Notre Dame classmates, Joe Adrian, was killed in Vietnam during a night scramble mission six miles off the end of the runway at Tuy Hoa on March 12, 1967. He was a shirttail relative of people my future wife, Mardi Morris, was in contact with. He was a cousin of her cousins.

I voted in the 1964 election while I was in London. In the fall of an even-numbered presidential year, you will have everybody from president to some U.S. senators, all members of the House, governors and everybody below that, and county officials on the ballot. The effect of that is to provide some community of interest in the nomination of the president. You want somebody at the top of the ticket who will help you in your state.

I applied for and got an absentee ballot as a student at the London School of Economics and brought it to a political science class. Those who looked at it were quite amazed at the number of choices Americans had. That is not the case in most of the rest of the world, including the United Kingdom. Their elections don't have the same predictability of the date the election will be held and which offices will be on the ballot.

Hughes was reelected in 1966 and two Democrats survived, Lt. Gov. Bob Fulton and state Treasurer Paul Franzenburg. They both served until 1968.

In 1966 on my way back to London, I stopped in Washington, D.C. and saw my godfather, Tom Kennelly. I had an interview with the board of governors of the Federal Reserve System. They made a pretty sincere pitch for me to come and see them when I got back from London in 1967. But I didn't go to see them. In the meantime, the war in Vietnam, teaching at St. Ambrose, and working in Harold Hughes' campaign took all my time.

There was an actor named Chaim Topol during the 1967 Arab-Israeli War. He's been in movies, including *Fiddler on the Roof*. He did a live stage presentation in London that I saw. As the '67 war began, he flew back to Israel after a Saturday night performance to fight.

We studied international economics and finance at the London School of Economics. The people in England, Scotland, Northern Ireland, and Wales still lived like they did after World War I. The depression of the 1930s had not ended for them in 1967. Why? Because of the wet blanket over the United Kingdom that was represented by the crown, queen, ruling class of three hundred or four hundred people who served in the House of Lords and owned a lot of the assets, another five thousand or ten thousand people who were knights and ladies, and people who inherited great wealth. From an American's viewpoint, it was like going to a place that was still mired in the Depression.

There was a stereotype of the rich American. We were rich compared with them. It was unbelievable. They had a monetary system that was based on pounds, shillings, pence, and half-pence. They had only recently retired the farthing, which was a quarter of a pence.

To Americans, it was like play money. You could get a lot for four pence, which was less than a nickel. For four pence, you could ride the subway for six stops. There were big heavy coins left over from 1901, 1910, and 1940. So that did not give Americans a very good reputation in England. We all seemed like we were enormously rich.

I had to play a very careful line; so did Jim Leach who came over as a student at the London School of Economics in 1966 and 1967. The post-World War II babies were tired of the class system, this wet blanket of privilege. That's what fermented the Beatles, Rolling Stones, and other British music, plus movies and the social life in the 1960s.

My tuition at the London School of Economics for each of those three years was ninety pounds a year or about $270 a year. The school was founded at the beginning of the twentieth century by the Fabian Socialists. The Fabian Socialists are best known for an Irish playwright named George Bernard Shaw. There was a place called the Shaw Reading Room on the fifth floor where you could go to relax.

The school played this iconic role in England of trying to shatter the class barriers represented by Oxford and Cambridge. So English, Scottish, northern Irish or Welsh students who came to the London School of Economics were buying in on shattering the old norms. They were among the most radical people on campus. They wanted to shatter the old norms even if they were born into very upper-class families.

At the London School of Economics we had a series of lectures from one teacher. They might have been only once or twice a week, but the lectures would be in a big hall with plenty of students. We were also assigned to classes. The weekly classes would have only eight to twelve students. Then there were tutorials, individual meetings with the teacher. So I had all three of those experiences at the London School of Economics.

My teacher in my first year was named Michael Oakeshott. Like O'Malley, Oakeshott was a well-known, highly regarded scholar who had worked in England at the London School of Economics for twenty or thirty years before I got there. He was highly regarded as a person who knew all of western civilization from the Greeks and Romans to the Middle Ages to the modern era. We had him for a series of lectures in the fall, winter, and spring terms.

The surprising thing to me was that he covered academic ground that I'd been introduced to in high school and again in college. Here I am in London, and we're going over the Greeks, Romans, post-Roman era, Dark Ages, Middle Ages, and modern era, including the eighteenth, nineteenth, and early twentieth centuries. It was a very electrifying experience. I enjoyed it immensely.

We also had teachers who discussed the early version of what became the Common Market that resulted from the Marshall Plan. There was something in Europe called the Six. The Six were countries that united in a treaty. Later they became the Common Market. England was not part of the Six. The Six were countries like France, Belgium, and Italy that used the romance languages and then more countries like Germany that did not use the romance languages and were not Catholic.

A storied visitor came to the London School of Economics five, six, seven, or eight times every school year as part of their three or four days in London. It was in this tiny neighborhood not far from downtown London. It was called Houghton Street, Aldwich and located not far from the Inns of Court, a very famous place where the lawyers gather in London. It was not far from St. Paul's Cathedral on one end and Westminster Abbey on the other.

One speaker was at the American Embassy. I went down to the embassy one day to do something with my visa or passport. I saw a crowd of journalists; there was a reporter from the *New York Times* and another reporter from the *Washington Post*. I asked, "What's going on?" They said, "Robert F. Kennedy is here." So I stayed. Kennedy emerged out of a crowd of about fifteen or twenty people, walked right over to me, and shook hands. I was kind of astounded. By that time he was a U.S. senator.

———

Speakers frequently would appear at 1 p.m. at the London School of Economics. Everybody on campus knew who the speakers were each day. Almost everybody on campus walked through the main building every morning. One of the speakers was Malcolm X. He was this black American.

Malcolm X was terribly popular among the Third World students at the London School of Economics. They all knew who he was. Then 75 or 80 percent of the students were students from the United Kingdom. He was more of a matter of interest to them – almost like a curiosity although he played to a theme they loved, which is "the Americans are not perfect."

In other words, there was a common mind-set, "Well, yeah, you might think you won World War II, set up NATO, and all the rest. That's what you think. But, you know, we're not just nobody."

So when Malcolm X looked at the crowd, he was looking at this group of up to four hundred students. He gave the same opening every time. He'd smile and say, "Brothers and sisters." I understood what he meant. But especially with the students from the British Isles, there was kind of a ripple of laughter. That surprised Malcolm X. He thought and did kind of a double take.

The African, Middle Eastern, and English-speaking students from South and Central America related completely to Malcolm X. They didn't think it was funny. Once the ripple of laughter ended, he got his remarks going again. His remarks centered on colonialism as a bitter and tragic infliction of the Europeans and Northern Europeans on a lot of the rest of the globe.

If you think of the years 1964 through 1967, what he described so encompassed Americans ramping up the war in Vietnam for what could be viewed by some as the best of motives. For people who had lived in a colonial world, the war in Vietnam was an attempt by Americans to impose their rule in place of the French, British, Belgians, Germans, and Italians. The World War II and Korean War generations just didn't see it that way.

That was not hard for me to live with. I could walk back and forth between those arguments. I was not the only American who could do that. On the whole, we were opposed to the war in Vietnam for our own reasons. It was a very vivid experience.

Not long after Malcolm X spoke at the London School of Economics, he went back to the United States. He was assassinated within ninety days of his remarks at our school. In London, England, the Third World students were outraged. They stormed around the place the day the news came out. From their viewpoint, the Americans killed him. I thought, indeed, that's the way it's viewed around the world.

The African American moviemaker Spike Lee uses quotes and pictures of Malcolm X and Martin Luther King Jr. at the end of one of his 1990s films, *Do the Right Thing*.

Another person my age was Cassius Clay. He had changed his name to Mohammed Ali. Ali was very big in my life because of his boxing prowess, resistance to the Vietnam war, and resistance to the draft.

I really liked the Beatles' music. They played live in London, but I never saw them. If I'd known how to see them, I could have seen them. I was never able to negotiate the announcement about a concert's time, how to get tickets, and then go, get the tickets, and be admitted to the concert. So I was very conscious of the Beatles. I was also conscious of the Rolling Stones, who were very big then. In fact, Mick Jagger had spent one year at the London School of Economics before I got there. That was always noted in the descriptions of him at the time. The women in his life floated all across popular culture for the next thirty or forty years. I never saw the Rolling Stones perform though.

The third person who came through London was Bob Dylan. Dylan was accompanied by none other than Joan Baez. Culturally, the Bob Dylan/Joan Baez visit made a big splash when I was in London. All of that was happening, and I was very conscious of it.

My first cousin, Pat Curoe and his bride, Neva Jean (Nege), were married during the summer of 1967 at the Air Force base in Omaha, Nebraska. At Christmastime in 1964, I was in London, so I went down to Spain and spent Christmas with Pat and Nege. She was the daughter of an Air Force colonel.

One of the women cousins in the family said to me at Pat and Nege's 1967 wedding, "You waited too long. All the good ones are taken," meaning I couldn't find someone nice to marry. I replied, "Well, Pat, who's about eight months older than me, found somebody nice." She replied, "Well, Pat's Pat."

But it was true that in 1967 I was already twenty-five years old. It was true that in Davenport and the Quad Cities the most attractive girls I met were already married to other members of the St. Ambrose faculty.

Walter Bagehot was a nineteenth century Englishman who wrote a book called *The British Constitution*. The book discussed the British Constitution going back to the Magna Carta. The Constitution is more a compilation of things that have happened over centuries. So Bagehot described all of that in his writings in the nineteenth century. He had this brilliant insight that endures to this day. There were the dignified parts of the Constitution and the efficient parts of the Constitution and the British government.

The dignified parts are represented by the queen, royal family, House of Lords, and iconic capitol with Big Ben, the tower clock. The dignified part of the Constitution is the part that keeps the population loyal, so to speak: the queen coming in once a year and reading the queen's speech, the House of Lords with their costumes, and the script dating back three or four centuries. The efficient part is that portion of the government that actually governs. It is the House of Commons, prime minister, cabinet, and civil service.

In the United States, you do not have that easy division. The president of the United States is both the dignified part and efficient part. The president may not have the powers of a king, but the queen has no power. She has to do what the efficient part tells her to do. In Washington, D.C. the president is head of government and head of state. In Britain, the prime minister is head of government, so the king or queen is the head of state. The prime minister does not dress in fancy clothes; the prime minister runs the government with the civil service. The prime minister and cabinet make the decisions.

There were huge arguments in the 1960s about whether there was a presidential government or prime ministerial government in the United Kingdom. That distinction made by Bagehot in the nineteenth century makes sense of a lot of things that happen in the United Kingdom and in this country.

Co-author's note: Malcolm X, born Malcolm Little, was born in Nebraska in 1925. He lived in various places, including Milwaukee, Flint, Michigan, and Boston to name a few, before moving to New York's Harlem neighborhood in 1943. His father was a Baptist minister. Malcolm first seriously was introduced to The Nation of Islam by several of his siblings who wrote to him while he was in prison in 1945.

CHAPTER 6

LAND COLLEGE JOB

Visit with **DEPARTMENT CHAIRMAN** pays off; brother lives through Tet Offensive.

When I was in my senior year at Notre Dame, I was home, by good fortune, on the same weekend that our newly elected governor, Harold Hughes, was speaking to the Rotary Club at a noon luncheon in Davenport. I was invited to go to that meeting with Dick Kautz, who was a friend of my dad's and worked at the Davenport bank. (Dick became a longtime friend of mine, too, later in life.)

I sat next to a priest who had taught me in high school, Father Joe Kokjohn. Father Kokjohn was probably vice president of St. Ambrose College at that point. Kokjohn knew that I was finishing at Notre Dame, and he also learned later that I was going to the London School of Economics the next three years after Notre Dame.

When I got back from London in the summer of 1967, I didn't know what I was going to do. It was either go into the Navy Officer Candidate School in late November or early December, or I didn't know what else. Maybe the Selective Service draft would put me in the Army for two years.

The next morning after Gerald O'Keefe from the Minneapolis-St. Paul area was installed as the new bishop, Father Kokjohn called our house and asked my mother, "Is Pat around?" She said, "Yes," and I got on the phone. I was kind of desperate at that point not knowing what I was going to do next. He said, "Come over to St. Ambrose and we'll talk about what you're going to be doing in the fall."

I went over to St. Ambrose and Father Kokjohn typed out a letter to Father Sebastian Menke, the president of St. Ambrose, that included what I'd studied at Notre Dame, what I'd studied at the London School of Economics, and if he was interested, I would be interested in a job teaching economics at St. Ambrose. I signed the letter.

The next day, the chairman of the department, Gerry Hamel, called me and asked me to come over for a visit. So I went over to talk to Hamel and told him what I'd studied and what I'd taken my exams on at the LSE. He said, "Do you think you can teach these classes at St. Ambrose this fall?" I said, "Yeah, I can easily teach these." Just like that, they cranked out a contract. I went over and met Father Menke. I said, "You know, I still have the draft board to deal with and the Navy."

St. Ambrose went to great lengths with the governor's office and the director of the Selective Service for the state of Iowa to make the case it didn't have teachers qualified to teach these courses because the war is draining off graduates of colleges and universities that could teach these courses. Within two weeks of me signing that letter to apply for the job, I had word that I was not going to be drafted and I did not have to go into the Navy in December.

My brother, Bob, who had gone into the Army based on his ROTC training, already had twelve months under his belt as a first lieutenant. He got his orders in the summer of 1967 to go to Vietnam as I was being exempted from the draft. My brother was not resentful in any sense. My brother and I were very close.

Like most noncareer military people I met then and for the next five decades, Bob had a very realistic view of the United States Army. One, that they would receive a lot of free training and see a lot of expensive things in North America and Southeast Asia in the form of tanks and planes. Second, the Army is a very human institution filled with people who sometimes are heroes and saints and sometimes are greedy, sinners, and very unreliable. The war in Vietnam was very fraught. It was intense and filled with emotion and hard for those involved to gauge who to trust.

Bob lived through but could have lost his life in the Tet Offensive of early 1968 in South Vietnam. He told stories about how when you were out on patrol around Saigon away from a military base, your life was greatly at risk. You could be killed by ambush or by Vietnamese inside your own vehicle. You never knew if you were going to be killed or maimed. The camp, which had around nineteen thousand soldiers, had a perimeter surrounding it that the American military aerially defoliated. Helicopters sprayed poisons that knocked down the jungle growth so that the camp theoretically was safe.

Bob would say, "We'd be in the camp with these big cookouts and you'd be showering while they were defoliating. They were spraying chemicals right on you and right on your steaks from the sky in order to protect you from the Vietnamese."

He came back from Vietnam at the end of June in 1968. He said that coming home, they were stockpiled on planes and sitting on long benches arm-to-arm, backs to the walls of the planes, unsure if they were going to be attacked one more time as they flew back to the States. They were flown to the West Coast and dumped out at some major air base in the state of Washington. Each soldier got a thirty-day leave and a ticket to wherever he wanted to go.

The American government's version of the Tet Offensive was that it was a huge victory for us. The Viet Cong and North Vietnamese attacked with all they had and we wiped them out. But that's not what it looked like from the United States population's viewpoint. They almost occupied our embassy. They had armed troops inside the perimeter fence. If they were capable of doing this, we were not winning the war. The Tet Offensive was the end of President Johnson's administration. Nobody could say with any certainty that we were winning in Vietnam.

My brother stayed in the military for another year or so and served in various places. When he finally was released from military service, he went back to De Pere, Wisconsin, and took some more courses at St. Norbert College. He even had a job there in admissions. He was playing out getting over being in the military for the better part of 2 1/2 or three years.

He got a job in Illinois state government heading up a Vietnam veterans outreach program. He worked for an agency called the Governor's Office of Human Resources. Bob was very good at it; he spoke the language of Vietnam veterans. He ran a program that hired Vietnam veterans to work in the afternoon and at night. He hired ninety or a hundred veterans to do this kind of work and worked in Springfield, Illinois, and Chicago. He met his wife, Camille, in Chicago while doing the job.

When the administration changed in Illinois, the directors above him replaced him. So he moved from the Chicago area to Iowa City and got a job with the University of Iowa Hospitals and Clinics. He rose to department head with three hundred or four hundred employees. Her served on a task force paid for by the Twentieth Century Fund that issued a report on the problems faced by Vietnam veterans: *Those Who Served*.

He got skin cancer in 1981 and died in 1983 in Iowa City. When he died, he was one of twenty-two thousand American servicemen who had the same illnesses. They started with skin cancer, then it metastasized into tumors on the brain within a couple of years. We think it was the result of Agent Orange. The *Chicago Tribune* published his obituary at the top of that page.

Robert McNamara, the secretary of defense under President Johnson, left the secretary of defense job and became head of the World Bank. By working to save lives through his efforts at the World Bank, McNamara was trying to atone for the damage to Americans and people in Southeast Asia during his tenure as secretary of defense.

I was already on Sen. Hughes' staff when President Nixon was forced to resign. Vice President Gerald Ford took over as president of the United States. Ford was unable to hold the line in Southeast Asia. The end of the war for Americans came at the time we saw the now famous pictures of helicopters flying off the roof of the embassy one helicopter after another.

Bob described that scene seven or eight years before it happened. He would say, "When we leave here, we're going to be leaving by helicopters flying off the roof of the United States Embassy." When that actually happened, it was eerie how easily he had described what the end of the war in Vietnam would be like. During his final illness in 1983, his wife was about to give birth to a baby girl who was born about five weeks after Bob died. Now she's happily married in Chicago with children of her own.

It took me one day to get all set as instructor in economics at St. Ambrose College. It was a great job for me. Number 1, I had worked over the subject matter for three years at the London School of Economics. Number 2, the student body was younger than me, but in another sense, my contemporaries. They were my contemporaries because they came from Iowa and Illinois and some from farther away.

Whether I knew their families or didn't know their families, I certainly knew the families of 10 or 15 percent of the students I was teaching. I didn't know the families of the other 85 percent, but I could identify with their families. They were the kind of families that sent their boys to St. Ambrose College.

In those days there was a girls' college nearby called Marycrest College run by the nuns, but our school was all boys. The administration at St. Ambrose included two priests. Those two priests had not been my teachers, but they were priests of the Davenport Diocese. They were friends of all the other priests who taught me in high school. So they were quite friendly to me. It was like having bosses who knew what I was capable of and confident that I could do the job.

My father had long been the electrical contractor who wired their buildings. So dad and the electricians knew the whole St. Ambrose campus, and I knew the whole campus. I had gone there to high school for two years at old St. Ambrose Academy. Getting that job was one of the huge, positive turning points in my life.

In the meantime, the country was entering the turmoil of 1967-68, which related to the war in Vietnam. The baby boomers were just coming out of high school and starting college. The student body only knew about the Great Depression from their parents and grandparents. The student body was much less respectful of government authority, of "the way things ought to be." The faculty at St. Ambrose had older people, so somebody younger like me could relate to all these students immediately. I really enjoyed the teaching job.

But what was hard for me was living in Davenport. The social life consisted of finding whatever single girls were around, which were few and far between. I sometimes took out girls who were four or five years younger than me, freshmen and sophomores in college. But they were from Davenport families and they had gone off to college a thousand miles away. They'd be home for the holidays and I'd connect with them. In retrospect, it was a very unusual situation. My closest friend was a man six or eight years older than me who wasn't even on the faculty; he was dean of students. But I got along. It was fine during the school year of 1967-68.

CHAPTER 7

BOBBY, MLK JR., & ME

UNFORGETTABLE assassinations of political, civil rights leaders in 1968 hit home.

During the spring of 1968, I attended an event called "A Salute to Iowa's Future." It was a major fund-raising dinner for Gov. Hughes' Senate campaign. Bobby Kennedy was there and had an associate with him who was a very distinguished lawyer, maybe four years older than me. I visited with that guy. He subsequently became a professor at Georgetown Law School in Washington, D.C. Peter Edelman has been a big player in a lot of the political developments in the last fifty years.

Not only did we visit that Friday night at the event, but also the next morning when Kennedy was leaving. We met in the Savery Hotel lobby by accident. We visited for about an hour while he waited for Bobby to finish phone calls and other things. They were headed for Los Angeles to pay a call on Cesar Chavez and the farmworkers. Bobby was going to walk with him and the farmworkers on one of their marches. It's quite unforgettable to me.

I met Bobby two or three times. I had met him once in London when he picked me out of a crowd at the American Embassy. He walked over and shook hands with me that day only because I was a young person in a crowd of press people and other hangers-on.

If Bobby Kennedy hadn't been shot, I've always thought he would have had a good chance of winning the presidency. But others who I've been associated with, Harold Hughes I think, and certainly Ed Campbell and many Democrats that I know around the country and here in Iowa, were positive that he would win. He was such an exciting figure. He had this historic unequaled ability to talk to both the working class white voter and the African American and Hispanic populations that are much more prominent today in national affairs than they were in 1968.

I felt terrible about Bobby Kennedy's death. I had this experience of seeing John F. Kennedy when he was a U.S. senator. My brother and I visited Washington in 1960 after I got out of high school. We saw John F. Kennedy give a speech on the Senate floor about the student loan program. I went to John F. Kennedy's funeral in Washington, D.C. – there was a ride going from Notre Dame to Washington. I hadn't met Bobby Kennedy at that time.

But at that time, a girl I knew at St. Mary's College, Arline Hagen, who was a year ahead of me, wound up as a governess to Bobby Kennedy's kids. I connected with her the day after the funeral in 1963 at John F. Kennedy's gravesite. She was there after it was all cleared out. Arline and I had dinner with my godfather, Tom Kennelly, that night. So I always felt that I knew the Kennedys more than I actually did.

In 1968 I was very personally committed to Bobby Kennedy's candidacy. When I interviewed with Dwight Jensen and Ed Campbell that spring of 1968, I conveyed to them I was so committed to Bobby Kennedy. It was Dwight Jensen who said, "Yeah, but you also want to get Harold Hughes elected, don't you?"

"Of course," I said, "I'm applying for a job."

I was highly committed to Hughes. At the same time, I'd conveyed a kind of passion for Bobby Kennedy. He lived for only one week after I was hired by the Hughes campaign.

———

I was in Des Moines at the Hotel Savery sleeping in the headquarters up on the eighth floor on the night Bobby Kennedy was assassinated. I lived through that experience with the rest of the nation. It's been played again and again, the shooting at the hotel in Los Angeles.

Hughes was going to New York City for Bobby Kennedy's funeral and Ed Campbell was going with him. I said I'd go on my own. So I went to St. Patrick's Cathedral for Bobby Kennedy's funeral. I wasn't in the church for the funeral, but I did go through the church beforehand, and I went by the coffin. Thos McDonnell, a friend of mine from school who lived in New York City, put me up in his apartment.

I believe Bobby Kennedy would have brought the Vietnam War to a quick end – I really do. I think President Nixon made a bad mistake continuing the war when people thought he was going to bring it to an end. The nation was transfixed by this idea of peace with honor. This was a way to say we could somehow get out of the war in Vietnam, not winning, and yet not feel like we lost.

I have an insight on that that relates to the work I've done on campaigns. Bobby Kennedy did not have a Bobby Kennedy watching out for him. John F. Kennedy had Bobby Kennedy watching out for him in the presidential campaign of 1960. Ted Kennedy could not play that role for Bobby Kennedy because Ted was already a U.S. senator. Ted's children or Bobby's children obviously could not play that role for Bobby Kennedy. He did have loyal people around him.

There's a man who played a role in Bobby Kennedy's life named Frank Mankiewicz. Frank Mankiewicz's father was Herman Mankiewicz, an iconic filmmaker from Los Angeles and Hollywood. Herman Mankiewicz produced the movie *Citizen Kane*. Frank Mankiewicz got into politics and was Bobby Kennedy's press secretary; he was the one who announced to the world that Bobby had died. Bobby died a couple of days after he was shot.

Frank Mankiewicz has a son who plays a role in the Turner Classic Movies Film Festival, and I have met the son and talked to him several times at the film festival in Hollywood. I have always felt close in that sense to the Kennedys.

While John, Bobby, and Ted Kennedy went to Harvard, some of their wives and sisters went to Manhattanville College of the Sacred Heart, then a women's college outside of New York City. Later, my wife, Mardi, went to Manhattanville.

I had a cousin, Pat Curoe, who was in the Air Force. He is nine months older than me. He was a graduate of Loras College in Dubuque in 1963. He got married in August 1967 in Omaha at the Strategic Air Command base to his wife, the daughter of a colonel. Pat, too, finished as a colonel.

When I went to that wedding, the chaplain who married them was a Catholic priest, and I said to him at the wedding, "You don't think the war in Vietnam is a good idea, do you?"

His answer was, "Well, there is no easy way to withdraw. We cannot withdraw without shame."

I thought to myself, I don't know, you're talking about shame, but we're losing thousands of men over there, and there is something shameful about that. But that was the view of the World War II generation at the time.

Martin Luther King Jr.'s death was very important in my life that spring of 1968. Martin Luther King Jr. is revered in one sense at Notre Dame. He and Father Theodore Hesburgh, the president of Notre Dame, are in a prominent picture on campus. It's possible there's even a statue of the two of them. On the other hand, Martin Luther King Jr. was quite controversial in 1960, '61, and '62. I was a very big supporter of King.

We have a long tradition in Davenport of the connection with the social justice ministry of the Catholic Church going back to the 1940s. There were two priests, Father Ed O'Connor and Father Bill O'Connor, who were on the faculty at St. Ambrose. Their nephews, Thos and Johnny McDonnell, were my close friends.

I grew up with that tradition that relates to very obscure issues from the 1940s – the labor movement, the Communists, the UAW. Then in the '50s it was the Hispanics and the African Americans. As the 1950s became the 1960s, it was a huge part of my life.

The loss of Dr. King was huge for me. It was like the country was spinning and everything was being overturned.

As President Kennedy took office on January 20, 1961, he was still dealing with the aftermath of World War II, Russia, Berlin, what was going to happen in Eastern Europe, and the Cuban missile crisis.

But the African American community in this country did not want to be told, "Wait; give us another few years before we address your issues." They thought they'd been waiting long enough. That gets discussed all the time in respect to Jackie Robinson, the baseball player; Joe Louis, the boxer; and school integration in the 1950s. All of that was very real in my life. I paid close attention to it because of the social justice education I received during my four years of high school at St. Ambrose Academy and then Davenport Assumption High School.

CHAPTER 8

IDA GROVE EVENT

SEND-OFF FOR HUGHES leads to feature in *Harper's* magazine, *Meet the Press* interview.

After the election in 1968, Harold and Eva were moving to Washington, D.C., and we had a send-off night in Ida Grove, Iowa, their home. It was cold so it was indoors. The local establishment organized the event. Behind the scenes, Ed Campbell asked Alan Baron of Sioux City to organize a northwest Iowa greeting committee. Baron loved that kind of thing. He was just relentless at it.

So he organized a northwest Iowa greeting committee to say goodbye to Harold and Eva on their way to Washington. Baron printed little badges with little ribbons on them. Everybody who agreed to be on the northwest Iowa greeting committee got a badge with a ribbon. All this is commonplace today, and I have boxes of badges and ribbons. But it wasn't commonplace then, at least for me.

Baron would go around to these counties and ask one or two people, and then they'd recommend some more. That was building the crowd. "Would you be on the northwest Iowa greeting committee?" he'd asked. He probably charged them fifteen dollars to be on the committee. This very big event in Ida Grove was packed with people wearing the ribbons.

Hughes, who was governor at the time, wanted his mother to come to the event. She lived in a nursing home in Fort Dodge. It fell to me to pick up his mother at the nursing home and drive her up to Ida Grove, which I was happy to do. He could always count on me. I heard him say once or twice, "We have Pat to do that." The point is, he did not want his mother, who was pretty old and subject to being a figure of fun, saying something incorrectly or looking like she was losing it. It was a sensitive assignment.

The editor of *Harper's* magazine in those days as Willie Morris, and that publication was really on the cutting edge. Almost at the last minute, Morris asked a favorite writer from his string of writers, Larry L. King, to do a profile on Harold Hughes. Maybe on the day before the event or that same day, the guy found out about it.

Larry King called and made arrangements to get to Sioux City. He had not done a single five minutes of research on Hughes. All he knew was what they knew: Hughes was governor for six years, and now he's been elected to the Senate, but we think that he should be somebody who gets attention. The writer arrived in Ida Grove, and I became his caretaker as well.

Hughes said right to his face, "You can ride back to Des Moines with Pat, but I want you to promise me you're not going to cover my mother. Leave her out of the story."

And King quite quickly said, "Yeah, no problem. I'll be happy to guarantee you that."

I followed by saying, "I don't mind talking if you won't quote my name."

He said, "Yeah, that's fine."

Here's the clue on who the guy is. He told me, "We all write for *Harper's*, but we all have our own lives. I live in Texas and I'm working on a play. I'm calling it *The Best Little Whore House in Texas*."

He told me about his play. Press guys love good stories, and that was the origin of that show. In fact, the title came from something he'd heard someone say. He could put in his play things that didn't need to be attributed in an interview. It could all be out there, so to speak.

There are two other things I recall about the send-off. As the evening went on, Eva was shedding tears. I thought it wasn't surprising. She was in the town where she grew up. They had lived in Des Moines for at least the last ten years, but Ida Grove was still home. I could recognize that from my family going back to Bernard and Dubuque County. That was home and where everybody knew each other. Eva wasn't sobbing loudly or anything like that. But as she sat there the tears streamed down her face. She was going to Washington. D.C. where she'd never lived and she was very uncertain about what it would be like for her family.

The second thing I recall was an insight by Larry King; it was the same one I'd had a few times when I was visiting other states. He explained that this event in Ida Grove was so comparable to numerous things he'd done in Texas. He could look around, and even though he didn't know anybody, he could tell who was the banker, the Catholic priest, the local mayor, the big shot who lives outside of town and is worth a lot of money ... he could just recognize all of that.

He said that to me that night driving back to Des Moines, and that's what his piece became. We all regarded it as the *Prophet From the Prairie* piece. It hit the newsstands on a Monday in March 1969. In a funny kind of way, it rocketed Harold Hughes up.

That Monday in 1969, the same day the piece in *Harper's* magazine hit the newsstands in Washington, D.C., the man who ran *Meet the Press* was over in our office. Bill Monroe was the moderator of *Meet the Press* at the time.

He said, "We want to do an interview with Harold Hughes on Sunday."

My role in that was minor because we had a press secretary and Park Rinard running the office. Yet, I did meet the *Meet the Press* moderator coming through the door. At the time, I watched the show every week.

The *Harper's* profile put Hughes on *Meet the Press*. Within a week or two, the columnists, who are a very small group who know each other but whose work goes nationwide, started this format: They'd do a column on something else and then put a couple of bullet points at the end. One of them wrote, "Watch out for a dark horse candidate for president coming from Iowa, Harold Hughes." The first time it happened, I didn't regard it as that big of a deal. Within about two weeks, it started showing up in column after column. These guys all had their own networks across the country in those days, so the idea of Hughes as a dark horse candidate was a theme that spread quickly.

Hughes and Park well understood that you could get out ahead of yourself too quickly, and it would destroy you. So when the *Meet the Press* appearance was being scheduled for the next Sunday, Hughes made a specific request: "Let's talk only about the subcommittee on alcoholism and narcotics." He'd just gotten the subcommittee assignment from Sen. Mike Mansfield.

In those days, the *Meet the Press* interview wasn't going to be the whole hour. It was just fifteen or twenty minutes at most. Hughes had been on *Meet the Press* before as chairman of the National Governor's Association.

The columnists thought Hughes would make a good candidate for president, and they thought he was thinking about running. The press releases that we took over to the Senate press room were lifting Hughes out of the group of senators who give speeches, chair meetings, and travel back and forth to their home states.

I remember as early as 1969 walking a press release over to the press office and the lower ranking people, including Connie Chung, who worked in the office, kind of laughed and said, "Hughes really hits Nixon, doesn't he?" At that point, I wasn't that confident dealing with the press, so I didn't say anything.

As for rumors about Hughes being a dark horse candidate for president, this was not my responsibility at all. Hughes' Iowa supporters, Joe Rosenfield, John Chrystal, Bill Knapp, and some others, paid for an office near the Senate Office Building on a private street called Ivy Street. The Ivy Street office was staffed by Baron, who had organized the guests at the Ida Grove meeting, and Eli Segal, who later worked in the Bill Clinton administration.

One of my friends, Paul Meagher, who lives in Washington, D.C., volunteered at the Ivy Street office. He was from Rock Island, Illinois and one year behind me at Notre Dame. We were friends and are friends to this day. We had this little operation going to collect information.

There were three or four or five others who got involved and worked there. They were exploring the idea that Hughes might run for president. We got the Ivy Street office organized in the summer or fall of 1969 or as late as January of 1970.

Co-author's note: The movie The Best Little Whorehouse in Texas *based on the play came out in 1982 and starred Burt Reynolds and Dolly Parton.*

Co-author's note: Meet the Press *is the longest-running program on network television, having debuted on NBC TV on November 6, 1947. The show has had only 11 permanent moderators in its 72-year history.*

CHAPTER 9

OFFICE ISSUE

LANDMARK ALCOHOLISM, narcotics addiction legislation passes after move to D.C.

When 1968 ended, the Hughes team kept me on the campaign staff while Park Rinard and Ed Campbell planned what they were going to do in Washington, D.C. It involved reshuffling the Harold Hughes team. Park had agreed that if Hughes was elected to the Senate, he would go to Washington, D.C. in the top job. I think Park really wanted to do that; he was giving up a job as head of the Iowa League of Municipalities. Park and Hughes decided that they would put Campbell in a senior position and call him special assistant. Campbell would deal with political matters with Democrats back in Iowa and around the nation.

That meant that Dwight Jensen, who was the administrative assistant, had to find a different title. They made him press secretary, which he accepted but could see Park moving in somewhat. Now Park had always been in that position of being Hughes' senior adviser, but only behind the scenes. Dwight was the top assistant in the governor's office. There were two or three other people including Wade Clarke, a lawyer two years older than me.

What were they going to do with the Des Moines office? Bourke Hickenlooper, the last senator, hadn't even opened an office in the federal building. He had kept an office going for twenty-four years, maybe in some law firm. Sen. Jack Miller had an office on the seventh floor of the federal building. Hughes was entitled to an office, which they quickly decided they would take and staff. So I would be put in that office. Lt. Gov. Bob Fulton succeeded Hughes as governor for seventeen or eighteen days.

As 1968 came to an end, they put me in Gov. Fulton's office, and I became his top assistant. But Jensen and three or four more guys and all the support staff in the governor's office stayed in the governor's office for the balance of Fulton's term. When Fulton's term came to an end, I moved over to the federal building with Gov. Hughes' top secretary, Ruth Yauk. We were on the seventh floor of the federal building, and Sen. Miller was down the hall in a different office.

I really didn't want to stay in Des Moines at that point. I had left St. Ambrose. I was glad I had gotten to work on the campaign. I believed several people around the campaign were recommending to Hughes and Park that they should keep me. One of them was banker John Chrystal, who was a nephew of Roswell Garst. He was enormously influential on Hughes' team.

For the first couple of months, there was no room for me in the Washington, D.C. office. Plus, there was a lot of talk in Washington that Hughes had overstaffed his Senate office with guys who came from the governor's office.

Truthfully, that was correct. Three or four of them were really good, but they each had to learn Washington, D.C. and U.S. Senate issues, which differed from the issues they managed at the state Capitol in Des Moines. Yet, none of them wanted to leave what looked like a rocket ship to the top. So I did get to go to Washington for a visit with the senator's top staff, and we had a good three or four days together. But I also didn't really want to stay in Des Moines. There wasn't an opening for me, though.

Eventually, a space did open for me, and I moved to the Hughes Senate office in Washington in March 1969. That's when I learned a student at George Washington University was also coming into the office every day. His name was Dan Miller, and he would make Iowa Public Television what it is today.

Dan died in February 2018. His widow once asked me to describe how Dan became so important in the Hughes and Culver Senate office staffs. I've always promised that I would try to piece it together for her. During the six years I worked for Hughes in the U.S. Senate, Dan Miller was this college student who would come in and work in the back room of this five-office suite. Hughes' office was first, then the top leadership, then the receptionist with a couple of secretaries, then my office with another guy and secretaries, and then the back room where they turned out press releases with mimeograph machines. Dan worked in there four, five, or six days a week. It took him the better part of six years to get a bachelor's degree at George Washington University, which isn't far from the White House. (Dan, Park Rinard, and I would work together later in the John Culver Senate office.)

In my role, I could deal with this very angry, emerging anti-Vietnam War constituency in Iowa on their terms. I didn't grasp it at the time, but Hughes and the top leadership of the office wanted it that way because they were Korean War and World War II people. They agreed with Hughes' positions, but it wasn't that easy for them to relate to this very vigorous anti-war group.

Starting in 1969, President Richard Nixon continued the war in Vietnam even though there was an idea he had a secret plan to end the war. Hughes had won the Senate race by 6,415 votes out of 1,100,000 votes cast. Hughes had run for the Senate in '68 based on advice that he got from one of his friends, a former governor of Wisconsin named Gaylord Nelson. By then, Nelson was serving in the U.S. Senate. Park Rinard and one other person went out to Washington, D.C. in the fall of 1967, visited Nelson, and asked Nelson if he had found the Senate to be a rewarding experience. Nelson and his staff people recounted that to me later on.

Park perceived that the Senate hearing room and the Senate experience to pass laws was very frustrating for Hughes. So Park did two or three things to ameliorate the problems that that posed for Hughes and to give Hughes something to get his teeth into. There was a series of privately-funded meetings in the Senate hearing room in the U.S. Capitol that were called the Crisis Conferences.

The Crisis Conferences were a 1 1/2-day-long meeting. A group in

New York City called the Fund for New Priorities, which included several millionaires and multi-millionaires, paid for them. They could afford it, and they enjoyed it. Hughes chaired the meetings, and panels were invited to come and speak. We'd invite other senators – Democrats and Republicans – to come to the meetings. The meetings had free-wheeling discussions around a big square table.

Some high-level people outside the Senate participated. They were of the caliber of John Kenneth Galbreath and Arthur Schlesinger Jr., two academics who had played a role in President John F. Kennedy's three years in office. The staff from the Fund for New Priorities came down from New York and actually worked in our office. Some of them were very sharp. This went on for two or three years.

Park Rinard's explanation of the Crisis Conferences was that we were giving Hughes something to get his teeth into, a give-and-take that was different from the Senate hearing room experience. It was an effort by Park to let Hughes be governor again with Hughes in control of the time. The Crisis Conferences represented a real problem to some of the other people on Hughes' office staff.

The Fund for New Priorities staff and the millionaires regarded Hughes' office and Hughes as being a real breath of fresh air compared with what they were used to when they came to Washington. For some of the people in Hughes' office, it was chaotic. They wondered how they could do their jobs with these people coming in and acting like they own the office. That perception did not apply to me. I could see that the kind of people who came to the Crisis Conferences as panelists were people whose work I had encountered as a college student and a student at the London School of Economics.

The press frequently covered the Crisis Conferences. It gave the press a chance to talk face-to-face with people they had known about for a long time. The conferences provided an alternative way to reach Hughes. There were five or six such conferences during the three years.

———

In 1969 Senate Majority Leader Mike Mansfield decided there

should be a subcommittee on alcoholism and narcotics and Hughes should chair that subcommittee. They could get office space for Wade Clarke Jr. when that subcommittee was authorized. Clarke was from Des Moines and had gone to the University of Notre Dame and the University of Michigan Law School. His father was a judge in Des Moines. Wade was moved out of the Senate office in the Dirksen Building to a different office. That's how I was able to move out to Washington – I took Wade's office.

Anyway, Hughes got the legislation drafted and passed in just two or three years. It was a huge accomplishment. The legislation set up an institute on alcoholism and another institute on narcotics addiction. It brought focus at the federal level to this issue. Hughes' military experience came to the forefront in the exploration of alcoholism and narcotics addiction. He mentioned that in his earliest hearings on the subject. "Is something being done to respond to alcoholism and narcotics addiction in the Department of Defense?" he asked. Since a senator raised that question, it got the Pentagon's attention.

It turned out the Pentagon did not have a very well established response to the issue; their programs were inadequate and not well known. Most military officers and enlisted people who had a problem with alcoholism were not addressed in a very professional way then. It was the same with drug addiction. It was the same way in the war in Vietnam; there was considerable drug addiction and a massive amount of alcohol problems. Hughes received enormous credit from the alcoholism and narcotics recovery communities for focusing on this and getting a bill passed.

A staff person for Sen. Edmund Muskie told me, "Hughes has accomplished an enormous amount on this issue in a relatively short time. Other senators work for years to get a bill passed. He got one passed right away."

Wade Clarke derived great credit for his work on that issue, too. He later earned an MBA from Harvard and became director of government relations for John Deere & Company based in Moline, Illinois.

John Culver and Dick Clark visited me during 1969 when I was in the federal building in Des Moines for about two months. John was a third-term member of the U.S. House of Representatives; Dick Clark was a former college teacher and Culver's top assistant in Iowa. They made an appointment in Des Moines with several people to talk about Culver possibly running for the U.S. Senate in 1972 against Jack Miller. Miller had won in 1960 and in 1966, carrying ninety-nine counties in Iowa in 1966. The governmental establishment in Iowa regarded Miller as being nearly unbeatable. Miller had taught at the University of Notre Dame Law School. When Jack Miller was introduced to a Republican convention in 1960, they played the Notre Dame victory march, which surprised me.

The story floated for the next couple of years that Culver probably would run against Miller. But as 1971 ended, Culver had not announced against Miller. In January 1972 there was still no announcement. My friend, Paul Ryan, received a telephone call and learned that if John Culver chose not to run against Jack Miller, Dick Clark, his administrative assistant, might. Ryan felt that would be a pretty big comedown; he did not encourage the idea.

But sure enough as January became February and there still was no Culver announcement, we all started to wonder. I had worked in the 1970 campaign for Bob Fulton and we were coming up to the 1972 campaign for governor and U.S. Senate. All of a sudden there was an announcement that Culver would not run against Miller. I believe the next day Clark announced he was running against Miller. There was another candidate named Nick Johnson who had been a highly-publicized Iowan and served in President Lyndon Johnson's administration.

Clark had a visit with a guy I knew well, Tom Higgins. He was from Illinois and came to Davenport to go to St. Ambrose College in the mid-1960s. Higgins' uncle, Monsignor George Higgins, worked at the United States Catholic Conference in Washington, D.C., an organization that represents the bishops across America. Monsignor Higgins was widely regarded as a champion of the social justice message of the Catholic Church. Tom Higgins was president of the student body at St. Ambrose, worked as a neighborhood organizer in Davenport, and lived on the crest of a hill in Davenport near what was then Davenport High School.

Tom Higgins suggested to Dick Clark that Clark walk across Iowa as a campaign gimmick or starting point. Both Tom Higgins and Clark told me their account of the walk. Somebody else had done it someplace else in America. In Illinois, Democratic gubernatorial candidate Dan Walker walked across the Land of Lincoln in 1971 and later became governor for one term.

The message that Tom Higgins and Clark got was if you're going to do the walk and you hang the press on that, don't distract from it by flying around the state to big events and doing press releases from the events. Make the walk the story that people follow.

And that's what Clark did. It became an unbelievably persuasive narrative that ran along the lines of "Dick Clark walked into Fort Dodge today and said …" By the fall of 1972, Hughes sent me back to Iowa to work in a governor's race. I came out just after Labor Day to work for Paul Franzenburg, the Democratic candidate for governor.

Above Franzenburg and Gov. Bob Ray on the ballot were Republican Richard Nixon and Democrat George McGovern for president. Nixon won forty-nine states in 1972. Then on the ballot were Dick Clark and Sen. Jack Miller; the congressional candidates; and the candidates for statewide offices.

When Clark finished the walk ten days before Election Day, he had walked the whole state. His press release said, "Dick Clark will continue to walk across Iowa and meet Iowans face to face." Politicians such as John Culver and myself and all kinds of other people laughed about that for the next few years. The walk provided an enormous press release opportunity. The walk was wildly successful.

Even though Nixon was carrying Iowa and Democrats were losing several other races, the Dick Clark race was enormously successful. Democrats did not win the Iowa House or Iowa Senate, but made significant gains. Then Democrats won the Iowa House and Senate in 1974.

The '70s exploded with the documentary *Woodstock*, the Beatles and Rolling Stones, and the war in Vietnam. Somehow Dick Clark's

1972 victory harnessed all of that with his walk across Iowa and Jack Miller's significant loss in the Senate race.

Paul Franzenburg in 1972, like Bob Fulton in 1970, was not successful in knocking off Gov. Ray. This was my third statewide campaign and turned out to be great preparation for the 1974 Culver-for-U.S. Senate campaign.

This cartoon by Pulitzer Prize-winning cartoonist Frank Miller reflects the two sides of issues that arose in the Iowa Senate in 1979. On one hand, Iowans for Tax Relief and others who favored cutting federal spending called for a constitutional convention. After a snowstorm shut down Interstate 35 near the Missouri border, however, many people wanted the federal government to send lots of money quickly for disaster relief associated with the storm. Published courtesy of the *Des Moines Register.*

WHAT A DIFFERENCE SOME SNOW MAKES!

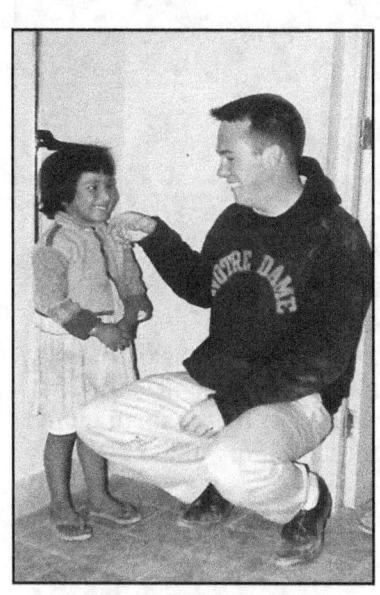

Pat Deluhery meets a girl from Lima, Peru during an eight-week stay in that country in the summer of 1962 as part of Notre Dame's global initiative. Notre Dame still is the headquarters for the Council for the International Lay Apostolate. During his stay in Ciudad de Dios, he met the Cardinal archbishop of Peru, the president of Peru, and the papal a nuncio.

The Davenport Assumption High School senior class officers including Pat Deluhery, second from right, were featured on the front page of the *Knight Beacon,* the school newspaper, on May 31, 1960. Graduation Night was held on June 5, 1960.

Knight Beacon

Vol. I—No. 2 Assumption High School, Davenport, Iowa, Sept. 25, 1958 4 Pages

Editors Select Winning Name For Paper; Pat Deluhery Wins Lifetime Subscription

Knight Beacon will replace the question marks used as the flag of the first issue of the school newspaper.

Pat Deluhery '60, a journalism student, captured a lifetime subscription to the school paper as an award when his entry in the "Name The Paper" contest was judged best out of approximately 250 names submitted.

When queried as to how he happened to choose the name, Knight Beacon, the fledgling journalist stated that "the first part of the name was inspired by the team's nickname 'Knights', while the second part, 'Beacon', seemed to symbolize the paper's ten policies and as a name to be lived up to." He dreamed up the "night-time pun" during a study hall.

Entries were judged by the four editors — Jim Murphy, Mike Gnam, Pat Knight, and Virginia Hagen — on the basis of originality, suitability and meaning.

Pat Deluhery, '60

The naming of a winner brought to a close more than a week of voting. Entries were written and submitted in the student cafeteria where a poster made by Kathy Mohr was displayed by promotion manager Marilyn Meisenbach. Staff artist Dick Craig drew the new flag for the front page.

"This name is, in itself, symbolic of the paper's Christian ideals and standards," asserted Fr. William F. Wiebler, advisor of the journal.

Editor Murphy stated that the beacon in the night seems to indicate the "light of truth dispelling the darkness of ignorance."

Associate editor Gnam liked the fact that "the name is symbolic and meaningful instead of merely being clever and witty as many of the entries were." (Examples of other entries: "Knight Mare"; "Quadrangle"; "Mother Goose's Goodies"; "The Assumption Gazette".)

Associate editor Knight thought the name reflected qualities of fairness, chivalry and Christian principles because of the ideals of knighthood implied in "Knight". Virginia Hagen, news editor, pointed out that the name referred not only to sports but also to scholarship. Moreover she

YCS Begins Activities This Week; Starts Selling Books In Cafeteria

As the Young Christian Students begin their first year at Assumption, six groups which operated at St. Ambrose last year are being reactivated, while Fr. Sylvester Conrad, assistant pastor of Our Lady of Lourdes parish in Bettendorf

ATTENTION

Pat Deluhery submitted the winning entry, *Knight Beacon*, in Davenport Assumption High School's Name the Paper Contest in September 1958. Deluhery said "the first part of the name was inspired by the team's nickname 'Knights,' while the second part, 'Beacon,' seemed to symbolize the paper's ten policies and as a name to be lived up to." He dreamed up the name during a study hall, according to a front page story in the paper on September 25, 1958.

Pat Deluhery is shown working in U.S. Sen. Harold Hughes' office in Washington, D.C. during 1969 to 1972. Deluhery witnessed several historical moments and events such as a letter from an Iowan about the secret air war over Cambodia during the Vietnam war, formation of the Midwest Caucus of Democratic Senators and Crisis Conferences, creation of institutes on alcoholism and narcotics addiction, and peace demonstrations.

Pat Deluhery, at right, talks to U.S. Sens. Edmund Muskie of Maine, Stuart Symington of Missouri and Majority Leader Mike Mansfield of Montana during a fundraising event at the Wakonda Club in Des Moines in 1973. U.S. Sen. Harold Hughes is between Deluhery and Mansfield. Deluhery accompanied the senators on the flight from Washington, D.C. to Des Moines and on the return trip to Washington.

Pat Deluhery, right foreground, confers with Iowa Gov. and U.S. Senate candidate Harold Hughes during a stop in Ottumwa, Iowa at the end of the 1968 campaign. Ed Campbell, who served on Hughes' staff, is facing away from the camera at right.

Pat Deluhery, left, and younger brother Bob, right, meet congressman Fred Schwengel in Washington, D.C. during a summer trip in 1960 after Pat graduated from Davenport Assumption High School in Davenport, Iowa that spring. Pat and his brother stayed with their aunt, Katherine Donovan, during their approximately three-week stay in the nation's capital. Then he and his brother spent another half week or so in New York City before returning home.

Pat Deluhery, left, chats with former Vice President Walter Mondale in Des Moines in 1983. Mondale represented Minnesota in the U.S. Senate from 1964 to 1976 and was vice president from 1977 to 1981. The Democratic presidential nominee lost to Republican Ronald Reagan in an electoral college landslide in 1984. Mondale became the oldest-living former U.S. vice president after the death of George H.W. Bush in 2018.

The Deluhery family as shown in about 1990: from left, Allison Deluhery, Rose Deluhery, Mardi Deluhery; back, Pat Deluhery and Norah Deluhery.

CHAPTER 10   LET'S NOT FORGET PARK

Rinard played big role in **TWENTIETH CENTURY IOWA**, ex-Davenport mayor says.

Former Mayor Thom Hart, my neighbor on Rushholme Street in Davenport, suggests that Harold Hughes and Park Rinard loom large in the story of Iowa in the twentieth century. My firsthand impressions of them and my experiences with them count for a lot. It's a story not told by other people the way I would tell it.

Park grew up in or near Mason City, Iowa, went to the University of Iowa in Iowa City, and probably majored in English literature. After graduating from the University of Iowa, he was associated with the well-known Iowa artist Grant Wood. By the account Park gave me later in his life, he worked for Wood for about four years up to the time Grant died.

Wood was quite controversial. His life has been the subject of one big book, *Grant Wood [A Life]*. That book slighted Park, who showed me the lengthy piece he wrote about Wood that ran in the *Des Moines Register* before the book was published. The book said Park never wrote anything more about Wood. I wrote a letter to the *Register* with a big self-portrait of Wood that was picked up in Iowa City, and there was a big one-day event in Iowa City later on.

The book's author, R. Tripp Evans, made several appearances in Iowa when he published the book. It surprised people that for as iconic as Grant Wood's famous painting *American Gothic* is and all the attention the painting received throughout the twentieth century into the twenty-first century, nobody had written a book about Grant

Wood until fairly recently. Park gave me an explanation for that. He said that whether it's Grant Wood, Irish author James Joyce, J.D. Salinger, or anyone else, they want the focus to be on their work. They don't want someone rummaging around in their life to try to figure out which argument they had with another person or whether they got along better with their father than their mother. Park and I discussed it enough that it made sense to me.

The time after the success of *American Gothic* when Wood moved to Iowa City and was associated with the University of Iowa has been the subject of a lot of speculation and academic work. He wasn't hired in the art department; he was hired in a different department. He was there for three or four years and maybe had a brief marriage to someone who was older. That marriage broke up. At a certain point Park engineered Grant's summers in northern Iowa where Grant could work on his art and produce three or four more very good paintings.

From Park's perspective, the East Coast critics immediately wrote a piece about Grant Wood that he died in despair and never had lived up to the potential people saw in him. From Park's viewpoint, Grant didn't die in despair. He was struggling in the last forty-eight hours of his life, and then he died. Grant was a happy man and he produced some pretty memorable paintings along with *American Gothic*.

The image of *American Gothic* with the older man, the younger woman, and a farmhouse window that looks like mock Gothic art is still used by cartoonists and satirists. It never goes away. That has made Grant's art very valuable, but not much of it comes on the market.

When we got to the Senate office in Washington, D.C. in 1969, Park had several of Wood's line drawings posted around the office to make people from Iowa feel welcome. They were a frequent source of conversation. So that's the Park Rinard I met when I was hired by Hughes' campaign in 1968.

Park had gone into the Navy during World War II and served in the San Francisco area. When he came back from the war, he went back to Mason City. After the war he also did what relatives of mine and other people did – made money by building and selling houses because there was a pent-up demand for housing. He moved his family to Des Moines in about 1957 when Herschel Loveless was elected governor in 1956. Park was one of just two professional people Loveless had on his staff.

After World War II the next generation of families had many children. There were a lot of families with four to fourteen children, plus the wives did not work outside the home. The husbands made enough money so that the wives could be the head of the household and run the burgeoning family. In those days we had fifteen or sixteen cities that were significant in Iowa. People were moving from the farms into town. State government refused to address the needs of these growing municipal areas.

So, what did Park Rinard do after Loveless lost the U.S. Senate race in 1960? He'd say, "I needed a job." He had a wife and children. His first job after the governor's office was with the City of Des Moines. He worked in City Hall downtown on the east side of the Des Moines River. Then he became director of the League of Iowa Municipalities, a position he held until the end of 1968. One of his biggest accomplishments was advising Commerce Commissioner Harold Hughes how to win the Democratic primary in 1962 and be elected governor in 1962, '64, and '66. There was a tribute to Park in Des Moines that I attended maybe just after the 1992 election.

Park had worked for Sen. Harold Hughes, Sen. John Culver, and congressman Neal Smith from 1969 to about 1993.

CHAPTER 11

NIXON UNDER FIRE

MIDWEST Caucus includes big players; Nixon's China trip adversely affects farmers.

Joining Hughes' Senate staff in Washington, D.C. in 1969, I saw him tackle historic issues. Park Rinard told me that those of us who worked for Sen. Hughes would be engaged in more challenging assignments than the staffers in almost any other Senate office. He was right. I believe that in decades to come, historians who describe America in the 1970s will encounter Sen. Hughes' work on a number of important issues. As a matter of fact, his work was even noted by journalists writing contemporary accounts of the period.

During the first four years Hughes served in the U.S. Senate, he and Park Rinard launched a very specific, pointed criticism of President Richard Nixon and the Nixon administration. It was frequent, once or twice a month. Sometimes it would be three or four times in a month, but it was just relentless. Hughes thought that Nixon was dishonest. He thought that from the start, and he hit Nixon for overturning some of the Great Society initiatives. Also, the choice of Spiro Agnew for vice president was offensive to Hughes, who knew Agnew from the governor's association.

Hughes cooperated with and worked on some of the things Nixon did in 1969, '70, '71, and '72 that came through Congress, including the alcoholism issue. In our office Wade Clarke was staffing the alcoholism and narcotics subcommittee. I worked more on the issues that came through the Committee on Labor and Public Welfare and the Committee on Banking and Currency. So we worked on a lot of big bills such as occupational safety and health, which was passed.

One of the earliest outreaches to services for persons with disabilities was passed. The chairman of that subcommittee was Sen. Jennings Randolph of West Virginia.

I knew about Daniel Patrick Moynihan, and I knew he was working in the White House. His prominence later on led to this revelation to me and others that Moynihan was pitching an idea at Nixon that he could be a modern-day Benjamin Disraeli, a nineteenth century British conservative prime minister who ushered Britain into the twentieth century by dealing with the social issues in nineteenth century Britain. Nixon seems to have gone along with Moynihan's idea while also playing this very dark role in politics.

Park Rinard pretty much stayed in our office. It was Hughes' job to go over to the Capitol, vote and talk to other senators when they were in session. There was a little apartment across the street where Park could get away from everybody and write. I'd often walk across the street to Park's little apartment office, get what Park had written down, walk all the way to the Capitol to show Hughes, and walk it back to our office. We were constantly doing that kind of thing. It's always hard to describe this or characterize this if you're in the middle of it. It wasn't that I was writing the words or even doing a very big job critiquing it. On the other hand, I was the one who'd get Hughes' immediate reaction on things and carry them back to Park. So there was that kind of a communications function for me.

As 1972 came to an end, Park thought that Hughes' reelection chances were severely crimped by Hughes' relentless criticism of Nixon during 1969 to 1972. So we stopped issuing critical press releases of the Nixon administration and Nixon himself. It was noticed. Once or twice Iowa reporters would comment on it to me. The president had already won this huge victory in 1972. The person who started criticizing Nixon's policies occasionally was our new senator from Iowa, Dick Clark.

In 1970 Hughes sent me out to work in the first campaign where I left the Senate staff and was put on the campaign payroll. I was going to work for Bob Fulton for governor for about seven or eight weeks. We were up in Sioux City with the candidate. There was a big stockyard there with up to three thousand cattle and an area for breakfast and lunch. It was a traditional campaign stop as early as six-thirty in the morning. The candidates would move around and shake hands. Two, three, or four candidates would work the crowd, and the crowd was big enough so that the candidates didn't get on each other's nerves.

So you'd sit at a table with four seats on one side and four seats on the other side. Somebody came in who was campaigning early in the morning. Her name was Dee Delaney Jepsen, Roger Jepsen's wife. Roger was from my neighborhood in Davenport and had quite a big family. He was a Republican and had a good career going on. I knew Dee Delaney because her dad was one of two brothers who had come from Dubuque County. And my father and mother knew the Delaneys in Dubuque. One of them was a close friend of my dad's. Roger Jepsen was considerably older than her. She was very attractive and a politician's wife to a T – beautiful and confident.

So I was sitting there and Fulton was out doing his thing. Dee is working every table. Finally, she got to me. She shook my hand and said, "What's your name?" I said, "I'm Pat Deluhery." And she did an immediate double take. I said, "I'm out here helping the Bob Fulton campaign." Her husband, Roger, was running for re-election to the lieutenant governor's job. Recognizing me, she just laughed and said, "I'll see you another time."

———

Roger Jepsen was more popular in the Republican Party than Bob Ray as they went into the 1970 election. Ray and the people around him moved immediately to get Jepsen out of elective office. Early in 1971, Marvin Pomerantz of Des Moines moved to dislodge Jepsen. Pomerantz was ruthless in a political sense in eliminating Jepsen from the Republican primary in 1972. And Pomerantz was successful. Jepsen even announced he was going to run for governor in 1972, but then withdrew because no one would support him.

From 1972 to 1978 Roger was back in Davenport with Dee. There was a restaurant north of Davenport called the Edgetowner run by a family named Holden. Edgar Holden later became a Republican state senator from Davenport. Edgar's brother ran the restaurant. Some time in the mid-1970s before I ran for the state Senate, I drove my mother out to Eldridge, Iowa for a late morning breakfast. We were at the Edgetowner that day and who was there but Roger Jepsen and his wife, Dee. We exchanged friendly words, and Dee was very gracious to my mother whom she had known most of her life.

Later on in 1978, we were both on the ballot from different parties: Roger for the U.S. Senate against Sen. Dick Clark and me for the state Senate from Davenport.

I was in the Senate chamber in 1971 when Hughes was asked to be the presiding officer. Congressman Culver came over from the House, sat next to Hughes, and talked to him for an hour. Hughes was not unhappy that Culver was visiting with him. I've always thought that this was the start of the events that unfolded the next year or two. In my opinion, John was asking Hughes, "Do you really think you'll run again in 1974?" If Hughes [had] said, "I haven't decided; maybe I will or maybe I won't," [then] somehow or another Culver thought "maybe that gives me a better chance to run for the Senate in 1974 rather than go against an incumbent, Jack Miller, in 1972."

So John chose not to run against Jack Miller in 1972; Dick Clark did run against Miller. Tom Higgins was a key advisor to Clark behind the scenes. Clark's victory presaged the Democratic Party resurgence in Iowa under the leadership of Clark and Culver from 1972 and beyond. Now, Higgins is on the board of directors of St. Ambrose University and lives on the West Coast.

In 1973 our office organized the Midwest Caucus of Democratic Senators. We had one Democratic senator from North Dakota, Quentin Burdick; two from South Dakota, George McGovern and James Abourezk; two from Minnesota, Hubert Humphrey and Walter Mondale; two from Iowa, Hughes and Dick Clark; two from Missouri, Stuart Symington and Thomas Eagleton; one from Illinois, Adlai Stevenson III; two from Indiana, Birch Bayh and Vance Hartke; and one from Ohio, Howard Metzenbaum. Hughes had a meeting in our office in the Senate Office Building in early January of 1973 where he invited all of those senators, and most of them came. Park and I were there as they walked through the door, and we were introduced to them in that sense. We didn't go into the meeting, at least I didn't.

Hughes proposed to them that we would work on agricultural and other issues that provided a critique of what was going on with regard to the Nixon administration. And they all bought in. From my perspective, these senators were big players on the national scene. Mondale became a bigger one later, but he was always recognized as being a very bright personality. And, of course, Humphrey had been on the Democratic presidential ticket in 1968 and in 1964 as the vice president.

We included Missouri but not Arkansas because it wasn't in the Midwest. I was present one day when Hughes was around some other senators, including William Fulbright or somebody like that from a nearby southern state. Hughes was trying to explain that we'd organized the Midwest Caucus because it was the Midwest; it related more to the crops than it did to political persuasion.

Yeah, I thought, that made sense, but Republicans were left out. I don't think he ever considered including Republicans. They thought it would slow down the critique of Nixon. That's what I think. Back in 1973 we had a Democratic senator from North Dakota. He was pretty cautious about what we did with regard to critiquing the Nixon administration. But he always went along with it.

A day or two later, Park and I walked around to each of their offices and made unannounced calls to meet whoever was their top assistant, who would be Park's counterpart. In those days, they were called administrative assistants and they got the top salary of anybody on the staff. They did not meet frequently, but they all knew each other and knew who Park was. By me meeting them, it communicated that "here's the guy who will come around." So we did that and then we immediately started doing joint press releases in the name of the Midwest Caucus, letting each senator issue it in his own state.

Each one of them would have a staff person fairly far down on the list like me in the position of giving advice on certain limited issues going back to the state. Park and I would convene a meeting of these people about once a week on Tuesday or Wednesday in a room near our office. They'd all come because they were getting so much good out of it back in their home states. We'd see what everybody was talking about and see what was emerging. Park was just a master at this; he could discern the technical side of an issue from the side that plays well to the press knowing the press aren't experts on all these issues.

The first issue that we really hit the ball on was President Nixon going to China six months earlier in 1972, well before the '72 presidential election. But Iowa farmers did not get the advantage of the deal that Nixon cut in China. It was just that simple. It was accurate because the big grain companies, traders, and people who were close to the secretary of agriculture, Earl Butz, were close to the insiders. And the insiders were close to the White House, Nixon administration, Department of Agriculture, and all that bunch. They tied up the markets for 1973 delivery rather promptly before the farmers and grain elevators knew this was coming. The people who didn't even live in the Midwest got all the advantage of it.

So we kicked it off in January or February 1973 with rather severe criticism of the insiders getting all the advantage of the China trip, and the people who were actually raising the grain and running the elevators were not in on it. They lost out and felt abused. That played well in all the Midwest states that were represented in the Midwest Caucus. So in these weekly meetings with the staff of the Midwest Caucus other issues emerged. It was a great spring with regard to those issues.

In the meantime, January through June and July 1973, the Watergate hearings had started. The national attention, and certainly the attention in Iowa, was greatly focused on the Watergate hearings. But from the viewpoint of the working press, not only at the *Des Moines Register* and *Quad City Times* but also at the weekly newspapers and radio stations, the things we were doing with the Midwest Caucus played very well.

In one sense, if the nation's attention and the major front page stories were on Watergate, you want to have something to cover and to do.

So around Iowa and the other Midwest states the noon radio station reports, the small town weeklies, and other smaller newspapers were picking up these releases one after another. It played because the releases gave them an alternative story to run for the people paying attention to them. It was to their audience. The releases played with a general theme: Somehow, people on both coasts and in Washington, D.C. learn about these things ahead of us, yet we're the ones doing all the work and not getting the benefit out of it.

Nixon had carried Iowa in 1968 by 148,000 votes. Hughes was the next name on the ballot, and he carried Iowa by 6,415 votes. Everything below us on the ballot pretty much went Republican. Bob Ray was elected governor, and the statehouse jobs pretty much all went Republican as did both houses of the General Assembly. Looking at the next two years, 1973 and 1974, we were trying to establish a narrative that already had been established over Hughes' previous ten or more years in elective office, four as commerce commissioner, six as governor, and four more as U.S. senator.

This would be the message: "You don't always agree with him, but you know where he stands." That was Park's angle to get that established in the state. Hughes was as good on this as well. Both of them had a very accurate and adept version of the electorate, which was that they didn't want to be reminded that they all voted for Nixon and he was now in trouble. You're not going to make any friends by saying "look how dumb you are." You just have to cut a different course. That was the course we cut with regard to the Midwest Caucus of Democratic Senators. In that sense, it was a masterful job that both Park and Hughes did. My part in it was to walk these papers that Park typed around to the offices and get them to agree to it. We'd get it done in a couple of hours.

I'd work all day in the office; I was very happy doing what I did during those years. On weekends, I'd often participate in the big anti-war demonstrations. Thousands of people would arrive in Washington, D.C. to march against the war. One of my friends from grade school, high school, and college was named Jim McGrath. McGrath and another friend of ours from grade school and high school, Jim

Anderson, had gone to the University of Iowa College of Law when I was at the London School of Economics. They graduated from law school in 1967 and went right into the FBI. By 1971 McGrath was working in the Justice Department for Attorney General Mitchell. Part of McGrath's placement in the FBI resulted from my godfather, Tom Kennelly.

We were marching down one of the main avenues in Washington, D.C. and walking by the Justice Department during one of the demonstrations. You could look up to the fifth or sixth floor where there was a balcony outside the office of the attorney general. The attorney general, who was convicted later during Watergate, was on the balcony. The assistant attorney general, who also was later convicted during Watergate, and the head of the criminal division, and McGrath were up there, too. I'm marching by with ten thousand of my best friends and associates. One of the troublemakers in the demonstration took a pop bottle and threw it at the attorney general, John Mitchell. They couldn't see the pop bottle coming toward them because they were looking down at the crowd.

But because I was in the crowd and looking up, I could see the pop bottle spinning up toward that balcony. I was really unnerved by it – I thought the worst could happen. Somebody could get killed up there. If that happened, somebody could start shooting down here. It was fraught with fear and emotion for people on both sides. The pop bottle did not hit the attorney general; it crashed on the brick wall maybe ten or fifteen feet away from him. They all jumped; I saw the pop bottle crash. They quickly turned and ran back into the building. It's hard to describe how intense the fight over the war in Vietnam was across the nation.

It was clear to me in the Senate office with Hughes that the receptionist would direct the protestors to come to me because I was the very young person, not of the World War II or Korean War generation. The older men in the office, senior to me, were from the Korean War generation. They certainly supported Hughes in his positions, but some of them were skeptical of the attitude of the young people who were so opposed to the war.

The Selective Service Agency was a World War II agency headed by an old general, Lewis Hershey. It had draft boards in counties throughout the nation that were wildly hated by many of the young people. The Nixon administration, however, was trying to renew the Selective Service legislation. Hughes was on the Senate Armed Services Committee.

One day Secretary of Defense Melvin Laird was testifying. I was behind Hughes; he often asked the question if I scratched a note or wrote a few things down. He asked, "Secretary Laird, young people regard the draft as a form of involuntary servitude." Laird resisted that characterization and gave an answer back. Hughes then was one of the people who led the fight against the renewal of the Selective Service draft. Eventually, the draft was terminated. It is hard to describe how passionate everyone was at that time. Again, we were losing ten thousand to twelve thousand servicemen a year in Vietnam.

The Emergency Employment Act came out of the Committee on Labor and Public Welfare. We were renewing the act. It was a way for government to spread money across the country and for people to get hired at entry-level, low-end jobs to keep the economy going. During a mark-up session of the full committee, Sen. Jacob Javits of New York asked, "Well, we want to say if they hire people at entry-level jobs at the state and local level, after a certain time they have to be promoted to something better." One or two senators spoke up and said, "I agree." And Javits threw back, "We can't just make these people into leaf rakers." *Leaf rakers* was a term going back to the New Deal, and it was derogatory.

Then Hughes suddenly spoke up in opposition, saying, "Jack, I can't agree with you. You know, when I was governor of Iowa some of the happiest employees around the statehouse were the buildings and grounds crew. Outside. Breathing fresh air. Not stuck at a desk drinking coffee all morning. It's a mistake to imply that a person is a failure if the job involves raking leaves." That was the end of the discussion. Everyone looked around and agreed with Hughes just like that. For me, the story describes the impact which Harold Hughes had on the Senate during the six years that he served there.

CHAPTER 12 — SECRET AIR WAR

Deluhery reads **EXPLOSIVE LETTER;** Waterloo couple's son killed by 'friendly fire.'

During the six years I worked for Harold Hughes, I frequently saw the letters. I did not open the mail – and I was not the first person to read the mail. People in the front office glanced at everything and put it in piles. But I saw many sensitive letters within an hour or two of them getting to our office.

One of the letters in 1972 was from an Iowan named Lonnie Franks. I got that letter about 11 a.m. one morning. The letter was addressed to Sen. Hughes, and it said, "We are bombing places that are not Vietnam." My recollection is that the planes took off in the Pacific Ocean and flew for an hour or two. Then Franks and other people working for the military would radio up to them and change the places on the map where they were supposed to drop their bombs. This issue became known as the secret air war over Cambodia.

I read the letter and thought, this is dynamite – I'd better take this right up to the senator. He happened to be in his office. So I walked up and laid it on his desk. I had not made a copy of the letter or anything like that. He picked the letter up and read it. I went back to my desk.

He got up and went to see Sen. John Stennis, chairman of the Armed Services Committee. Stennis had the letter by 1 o'clock that afternoon. Stennis took the letter; I don't know what happened after that. What we do know: That day a plane took off from Washington, D.C. to Vietnam and the commanding general in Vietnam was relieved of his duties. Gen. John Vogt, who flew on the plane, took over as commander of all forces in Vietnam.

Hughes mentioned it in his book, but I have a couple of things to mention that he didn't. One, a sweetheart deal was made involving the outgoing general, John Lavelle, who had to fly back from Vietnam. He was drawing flight pay and combat pay because he was in Vietnam, a war zone. But Gen. John Vogt, who relieved him of his command, decided that day that Lavelle also was disabled. So on his way back from Vietnam, Lavelle was flying back as a disabled soldier, which gave him a tax-free retirement. We all thought that was outrageous.

There was an Iowa couple named Peg and Gene Mullen, who were from a farm near Waterloo, Iowa. Their son, Michael Mullen, was serving in Vietnam. Peg and Gene were terribly worked up about Michael serving in this war zone, how dangerous it was, and how many lives were being lost. They complained about it, and then sure enough, bombs were dropped where Michael was, and Michael was killed by a bomb. We had heard from Peg Mullen before all this happened and knew who she was.

When the military informed Peg and Gene of their son's death, they said it was "bombs from friendly forces," meaning it was our own forces that dropped the bombs by accident. But it turned into the phrase "friendly fire." He was killed by "friendly fire." It sounds impossible. C.D.B. Bryan wrote a book about the Mullens' protest, struggles, anger, and resentment.

Friendly Fire became not only a best-selling book, but also a movie starring Carol Burnett as Peg Mullen, Ned Beatty as Gene Mullen, Dennis Erdman as Michael Mullen, and Sam Waterston as C.D.B. Bryan. The intensity of the war in Vietnam, the protests against the war, Johnson leaving office, three or four years of bloodshed – all of that is in the book and movie.

Before Michael died, Peg's anger over the war was expressed to members of the U.S. Senate and House. While I worked in Hughes' office, I took her phone calls before her son's death.

In his book, *The Man From Ida Grove*, Hughes didn't mention two more books on this subject. One was by Seymour M. Hersh called *The Price of Power*. The second was by William Shawcross called *Sideshow*. His book was particularly about the air war over Cambodia. Hersh in *The Price of Power* and Shawcross in *Sideshow* note Sen. Hughes' efforts to uncover the truth about the air war over Cambodia. Hughes' involvement in other legislative issues, such as opposition to capital punishment, alcoholism and narcotics recovery, and many others, is well noted.

CHAPTER 13

THE PERFECT WOMAN

LEACH'S INTRODUCTION, daughter's birth are significant events in decade.

The line "the search for the perfect woman" comes from a meeting with former state Sens. Bob Rush of Cedar Rapids and John Scott of Pocahontas. They had graduated from law school and were in Washington, D.C. when I was there from 1969 to 1975. Bob commented, "Boy, I've blown a lot of money." Somebody else in the group said, "Yeah, after college, I went down to Mexico and blew everything I had in savings and went into debt." Somebody else said, "I bought a car that I couldn't afford." Then they turned to me and said, "What about you, Pat?" I said, "Well, that's an easy one to answer. I've been in the search for the perfect woman."

I had already met my future wife Mardi, and we were dating. I had gone a lot of years after graduating from high school without meeting the girl of my dreams. That was godfather Tom Kennelly's line. He would always say, "Well, Pat, how are you doing on finding the girl of your dreams?" Tom was held up as a model to me when I was growing up by my father, especially. There was always this ideal that Tom Kennelly knew what he was doing and there is adventure out there.

My father's adventure when he was a young man was International Falls, Minnesota. There would be a power plant or a dam with electrical generating capacity three or four hundred miles north of Dubuque. So that's what had this huge influence on my life; try something, get out there, and do something.

Mardi and I met on a Thursday night in the early part of 1971 in

Washington, D.C. My father had died in January. Jim Leach called and said, "Pick me up. We'll buy ice cream and meet a couple of girls."

Jim wanted me to meet Peggy McMahon, who invited Mardi to join the group. We met at Peggy's apartment that night.

Over the weekend, I asked Jim to arrange a Monday night dinner at El Caribe in northwest Washington, D.C. I told him he should bring Peggy and Mardi and I'd meet them there.

What was it about Mardi? She was adventurous. She left home in Hawthorne, New York and moved to Washington, D.C. after graduating from college in 1967.

She was loving. She provided a home away from home for her younger sister, Jennifer, in a small basement apartment in northeast Washington.

She was committed. She clearly took seriously her commitments to her family and friends, especially her female friends from Manhattanville College.

Jim and I had been introducing each other to new female friends in Davenport, London, and Washington, D.C. since we first met after graduating from high school.

In September 1972, Sen. Hughes sent me out to work on my third campaign – this time, for Paul Franzenburg for governor. When I got back to Washington, D.C., I knew it was time to get married. Tom Kennelly laughed when he heard the wedding date and said, "There's nothing like a short separation to get you moving on an engagement."

Mardi and I set a wedding date of August 18 during the congressional recess in August 1973. We picked St. Joseph's Church on Capitol Hill. A historic property, the Alva Belmont House, was up the street from the church. Alva Belmont had a major role in the American women's suffrage movement. I asked the manager, Mrs. Chittick, if Mardi and I could use the house for our wedding reception and she agreed. Jim Leach agreed to be an usher and joined my brother Bob in wedding attire.

After our wedding, Mardi and I went to the British Isles on our honeymoon. When I came back, I found out Sen. Hughes was not running for reelection. We had all expected him to run for reelection. In the spring of 1973 Ed Campbell wrote a three- or four-page memo to Hughes that started off: "I know you haven't decided whether to run or not in 1974. But if you want to keep the option open to run in 1974, here are the things you need to do."

One was having a fund-raiser in Des Moines and inviting some of the highest profile people in the U.S. Senate to attend. Hughes said "yes" to that. So in May or early June of 1973 there was a big event in Des Moines. Campbell organized the event for Hughes. It was a typical fund-raising event. We had $1,000 tickets at the Wakonda Club on Fleur Drive and lower level tickets costing $25 or $100 for the big dinner at Veterans Auditorium.

I drew the assignment of flying with the three invited guests on a charter plane to the event. We left Washington, D.C. at 11:30 on a Saturday morning, flew to Des Moines, did the two events, and flew back to Washington, D.C. The three invited guests were Senate Majority Leader Mike Mansfield, Sen. Stuart Symington of Missouri, and Sen. Edmund Muskie of Maine.

Needless to say, it was an interesting day. Park Rinard said to me, "I'm not going to take up space on that small jet because two or three of these guys have very long legs." They wanted me to go because they wanted me to accompany the guests throughout the event and run interference. They didn't bring their own staff. I was it.

After we flew back from the event, two of them needed a ride home. We arrived at midnight or one in the morning. My car was at the airport, and the two who needed rides were Sen. Mansfield and Sen. Muskie. They lived not too far from each other in far northwest Washington. It struck me that night in listening to them how much their own families had to adjust to the life they led even though to the outside world it looked like all of the stuff was fairly easy.

But to Sen. Muskie and Sen. Mansfield, the challenges of handling family life and politics were very vivid. So from my perspective, I could only do it later because Mardi was immensely capable at handling her end of the package. To others it looked like "how do you guys manage doing all this?"

I thought Hughes was going to run again. I did not get married that summer just because of that but the two coincided. I had said to some journalists that spring, "Well, yeah, I expect to work on the campaign if he runs." Then they laughed at that and said, "Well, they all say they will run." I didn't disagree with that, but I thought maybe he will and maybe he won't. I thought when we did the event with Mike Mansfield that pretty much decided Hughes was going to run for reelection.

Anyway, I got back from our honeymoon, and we called home from New Jersey. I called my mother, and she said, "Do you know about Sen. Hughes?" I said, "No, what?" She said, "Well, he's not running for reelection." I was a little shocked.

But I had two immediate approaches from other senators. Sen. Vance Hartke from Indiana was the first. Within a week of us getting back to Washington, D.C., I was asked to visit Hartke at his office. He said he would put me on his staff if I wanted to join him. Then a few days later one of the staff guys of Sen. Gaylord Nelson of Wisconsin invited me over for a visit in his office.

When I got back to the office, I approached Ed Campbell and asked him what he thought about the two feelers I had received. Campbell said, "What's your rush? Sit tight. This is only September of 1973. We have another year and four months to go on this term, and you still have plenty of contacts in Iowa. Just sit tight." That was very good advice, and I'm very grateful to Ed for saying that.

So I worked on Hughes' staff for the next fifteen months, with the exception of working for John Culver in the 1974 campaign for senator. It was a tough race against David Stanley, who was making his third big attempt for office. Stanley had run unsuccessfully against Hughes in 1968. He had run in the primary against Fred Schwengel for the U.S. House of Representatives. And then Stanley came back to life in 1974 as the Republican candidate against Culver.

What clinched the deal for Culver was when President Gerald Ford pardoned President Nixon in the fall of 1974. It was just like the lights went out for all Republican candidates all over the nation. It was really comparable to 2018 when the U.S. House of Representatives went overwhelmingly to the Democrats.

―

In the spring of 1974, Mardi and I were expecting a baby and living in an apartment just west of George Washington University and just north of the Kennedy Center for the Arts. I was working for Sen. Hughes, often representing him at meetings with visiting Iowans.

That spring, congressman John Culver asked me to meet him in his office after a breakfast meeting with several Iowa congressmen and six or seven insurance company presidents from Iowa. When I got to his office, he asked me what I thought about his comments. I gave him an honest answer. They had come to lobby against no-fault auto insurance and a federal takeover of insurance regulations.

Culver had replied somewhat angrily that with the country facing historically high interest rates and the chaos of the Nixon administration's economic policies, he would have hoped they could have devoted some of their comments to the bigger picture.

In the privacy of his House office, I replied that the points he made were valid. But, I said, if I were a candidate for the U.S. Senate, I wouldn't have called their concerns "Bull ――."

Of course, he invited that response and knew before I spoke what I might say.

He walked over to the window and with his back to me, said, "Yeah, you're right."

I thought – then and now – my candid answer cemented our relationship.

John then asked if I could come to Iowa and campaign with him as I had done before with Senators Hughes, Fulton, and Franzenburg.

"Sure," I said, "if Sen. Hughes agrees and not before the baby is born this summer."

Daughter Allison was born on Monday, August 26 that summer. Mardi's mother came down from New York on Wednesday to help her daughter with the new baby. Ed Campbell had already left Hughes' Senate office in late 1973 to work on Clark Rasmussen's unsuccessful campaign for governor. Dwight Jensen had left. Bill Hedlund had left. Park Rinard was still there in Hughes' office.

On Thursday I flew to Des Moines and joined Culver's campaign in northern Iowa the next morning. A staff guy and three or four other people were traveling with him. It was about six-thirty in the morning, and John came in. He asked if they had remembered to bring his clothes from the dry cleaner. They had brought the clothes from the dry cleaner but the clothes were on tiny little wire hangers. John had an elaborate system with a leather hanger holder that worked if you were flying back and forth to Washington. They had forgotten to pick that up from the dry cleaner sixty-five or seventy miles away.

He took the wire hangers, bunched them up into a little ball, and threw them at Colburn Aker, who managed Culver's campaign office in Cedar Rapids. When I joined him in late August or early September, it turned into a good fit for John and me. I was challenged by him intellectually. I knew a lot of things that were helpful to him as we went from one town to another. I could always brief him on what to expect in the next town. He was a very good campaigner. He was highly motivated and enormously intelligent.

A funny story reached me on the campaign trail about the day of August 26, 1974. Culver, Rinard, several campaign consultants, and staff were having a big strategy session in Cedar Rapids that day. The usual subjects were discussed: spending decisions, staffing, and coordinating between Cedar Rapids, Des Moines, and Washington, D.C. Sometimes, Culver would raise his voice in frustration.

In the middle of the meeting, someone brought in a note and John started to smile, turned to Park, and said, "It's a girl, Park. They've had a baby and it's a girl."

Around the table, people wondered why Culver would care about a baby being born.

But, of course, to John it meant I could come through on my commitment to help the campaign.

I campaigned with John for a couple of weeks. Then John and I flew to Washington, D.C. and I drove Mardi and baby Allison to Davenport where they stayed with my mother through Election Day.

Who was the better campaigner, Hughes or Culver? John would always say there was "the other" about Hughes. What's "the other?" Well, "the other" is the unbelievable story of alcoholism and recovery, World War II, and six years in the governor's office with historic change in Iowa.

On the other hand, Hughes had a "detachment from all of it" as Park described it. What did that mean? Hughes had been through so much in life that he looked at all of it with a very detached, arms-length relationship. He was a very good campaigner and a very good speaker, but that detachment was a side of him that was more evident after it was all over. John and his wife were just a different package by far than Hughes and his wife Eva.

Shortly after our daughter Allison's birth and within a month or so, President Gerald Ford pardoned Nixon. At the time you couldn't see it, but there was outrage in America over that. Angry comments were made about that by the citizen on the street on the weekend that Ford pardoned Nixon. All around America people thought "he pardoned him?" In a way, I believe Ford got pushed into it by the special prosecutor. Otherwise, Nixon would have been indicted for a crime. Then you'd have a big problem if you were a Republican.

CHAPTER 14

MOVE BACK TO IOWA

TIRED OF SENATE, Deluhery lands St. Ambrose job after returning to Davenport.

Our oldest child, Allison, was born in 1974. She moved to Iowa with us in 1975 when she was a one-year-old. By the time I was elected to the Iowa Senate in 1978, Norah was born so Allison had a little sister born in 1977. Allison grew up with the life Mardi and I lived, which included fundraising events and events that attracted all kinds of people from the neighborhoods in Davenport.

There were pictures in the newspaper of four-year-old, six-year-old, and eight-year-old Allison running around the event. One of the people in administration at her high school, Davenport Assumption High School, said to me, "Allison observes everything that's going on and always knows what's happening around her." That's a good description of Allison; she was very observant.

In her high school years, we brought Allison to national meetings of various groups where I spoke or participated such as the National Conference of State Legislatures, which also had a State Federal Assembly. I would go two or three times a year to those kinds of meetings around the country including a big summer meeting when families were invited. I encouraged the people organizing the meeting to be sure they had some youth activities. Allison always seemed to excel at those youth activities. They'd have one group for kindergarten through eighth grade and a second group for high school kids.

Allison always did fairly well at meeting other kids and doing things like that. That introduced her to a wider national group and what it's like to be your age growing up in another part of the country. By her junior and senior year of high school, she looked at three or four different colleges: St. Thomas in Minneapolis, Minnesota; Notre Dame in South Bend, Indiana; and Creighton University in Omaha, Nebraska.

I had a meeting in the fall in Washington, D.C. when Allison was a senior in high school. That meeting was organized so people could try out ideas on state legislators to see if they were something that could be worked into a state or federal program. A lot of that was going on during President Ronald Reagan's eight years and President George H.W. Bush's four years. I said, "Let's line up some college visits, and you can come with me." So we lined up visits for Allison at Catholic University of America in northeast Washington, D.C., Georgetown University in northwest Washington, D.C., and maybe American University and George Washington University.

We made some phone calls, and there were people lined up to meet her at Catholic University and Georgetown. When we went to Catholic University, a young woman met us to take Allison around. Allison said as her visit started, "Well, Dad, I could go here." Sure enough, that's where she went. She graduated from there and so did Norah.

That proved to be a very valuable, important decision in Allison's life, and she has really prospered because of it. She went four years to Catholic University of America. During most of those four years she spent one or two days a week in the U.S. Senate doing things for Sen. Tom Harkin. She'd answer the phone, open the mail, and see how the system works. In the summer before her senior year of college, Harkin launched a big effort to have a staff of eighty or ninety college-age employees work in Iowa. Allison applied and got one of those positions.

So she spent the summer of 1995 working in the state living out of other places about half the time. They'd do things in campaigns such as knock on doors and line up volunteers. That paved the way for her to go back to Catholic University for her senior year. She worked in the Senate office again three or four days week. She was well known among the office staff and by Harkin. They hoped she would work in the campaign of 1996 for Harkin in Iowa. That's exactly what she did.

After school was out, she went back to Iowa and worked for Harkin. During the last week or two of the campaign, Harkin decided to send some of his people out to work in very tough legislative contests. We had a huge joint effort going on. Bill Clinton and Al Gore were on the presidential ballot; they were really coming after Harkin with a member of the House of Representatives. It was a very tough campaign, but Iowa was well known in Washington, D.C. by Bill Clinton, Al Gore, their top staffs, and the top staff of the party. We prevailed across the board. Harkin won his closest race in 1996. I won my closest race for the Iowa Senate in 1996 by 232 votes out of approximately 10,500 total votes cast on either side. My opponent asked for a recount, but it didn't amount to anything.

Harkin detailed Allison to my campaign during the last two weeks of the 1996 election. So Allison worked with me as we traveled around Davenport and Scott County. That was immensely helpful in keeping my spirits up. I recall on a Saturday afternoon I got a telephone call saying "Gore is coming to the Moline airport and he wants Allison and you to come to the event." We did that on the Saturday before the election.

So after the election, I said to Allison, "You know, you've already been abroad. If you want to, why don't you go to England right now and then come back?" She left in early December and stayed about three weeks in England reconnecting with a family I'd been friends with at the London School of Economics.

There was an Iowa personality in Cedar Rapids who was a member of the House of Lords in England. A predecessor of his was a member of the House of Lords who made this statement in World War I: Power tends to corrupt and absolute power corrupts absolutely. Lord Acton was married to a woman who was on the law school faculty at the University of Iowa. Lord Acton would go back and forth between Cedar Rapids and London.

So I encouraged Allison to send a note to the House of Lords telling Lord Acton she'd like to visit him. She and Pete Andrews' nephew were invited to go to tea at the House of Lords in 1996. Not unlike her father, Allison saw all of these people as being very down to earth.

Allison has never run for office. You can be close to it, know how it works and do something positive in your life that takes advantage of what you know, but chart your own course. Chances are that Allison has been asked to consider it in Minneapolis. I know when she was in college there were people who wanted her to run for office plus maybe work for them as staff. But in our family, the idea has always been to chart your own course and see what works for you.

Sometime during John Culver's 1974 campaign, we had a three-day visit by Sen. Ted Kennedy. The first event was in Sioux City where it was cold and rainy. Ted Kennedy was popular in Sioux City. A lawyer, Don O'Brien, was a big player in Sioux City. We were supposed to leave Sioux City and fly to Des Moines in a couple of planes. A reporter, James Flansburg of the *Register*, came to me and said, "I want to fly on the same plane with Ted Kennedy and John Culver."

I went over to John and said, "Flansburg wants to fly on this plane and not on the second plane." John and Ted looked at each other and said, "Well, maybe we'd better let him [Flansburg] do it." So I went over to find O'Brien in the crowd after this last-minute decision. I heard a voice behind me say, "Pat, stop." It was Ted Kennedy. He walked over behind me and said, "If somebody is to ask Don O'Brien to give up his seat on the plane, let me ask him." I stopped. Kennedy went over to O'Brien, came back, and said, "Tell Flansburg he can fly on the flight with us." I went over and told Flansburg.

Then I got on the second plane with O'Brien and three or four more people and flew back to Des Moines. When we got off that plane, O'Brien turned to me said, "You know, Pat, I'm a little disappointed that Sen. Kennedy and congressman Culver thought that he had to ask me to give up my seat. You could have asked me that." I said, "Well, yeah, I understand, but that's what they wanted to do."

The major portion of Culver's victory in 1974 was in his old congressional district. He won the race by about forty-eight thousand votes, but he won his old congressional district by forty thousand. That means he won the rest of the state by about eight thousand. That's the story then of Culver losing to Republican Charles Grassley in 1980. John could not keep the same numbers in his old district, and the numbers were not built up enough in the rest of Iowa.

In the spring of 1975, I was working in the U.S. Senate as a special assistant to U.S. Sen. John Culver. I was to be responsible for the Iowa operation: the three or four offices in the federal buildings, the employees and relations with various constituencies, the Democratic Party in ninety-nine counties, the trade associations with their statewide headquarters, and other citizen activist groups.

I played a role in an issue that came up in the U.S. Senate during January, February, and March, which concerned an appointment of Alexander Butterfield by President Gerald Ford to a board that regulated airlines and airports. Butterfield had worked in the Nixon White House and was responsible for revealing Nixon's taping system. Why Ford appointed him to that position and why the establishment in the U.S. Senate wanted to get him confirmed to that position has always been a mystery to me. But it's the way things work.

Culver decided to oppose that appointment, vote no on the confirmation, and make a battle over it in the U.S. Senate. It was a very big joint effort that was one of his first tries in the U.S. Senate to make an impact. The work involved asking two of his closest associates from Harvard and Harvard Law School who were in Washington, D.C. to assist him.

One of the men was named Rob Homet. He was not on the payroll; he was simply John's friend. He was widely connected, had this career from 1960 to 1975, and was widely known. The other, Fred Holborn, was on our staff, but that wasn't his only job. Fred also had a teaching position at Georgetown Law School. He floated back and forth five or six days a week between teaching and coming to the Senate office and serving as counsel to Sen. Culver.

Culver put his dissenting view in the report that advanced Butterfield's name out of committee to the full Senate. In working on that dissent, I brought up this point: We're mixed up because on one hand, we're saying this is a question of whether somebody who was in the military can now be on this board as chairman. On the other hand, we're going to overturn or ignore the law and confirm him even if the law says you can't be chairman of this board if you're a former military officer.

It became quite a struggle in the U.S. Senate on the day the confirmation came up. The suggestion I made when we were doing the dissenting opinion for the committee report was responded to by Fred Holborn. The way he put it was that these questions are not personal, they are institutional.

On the day of the debate and the vote, Sen. Mike Mansfield, the majority leader of the Senate, looked over the committee report, looked over Culver's dissenting view, quoted that line on the floor of the U.S. Senate, and decided to vote no on the confirmation. Just like that, the confirmation was turned down. It was Culver's first big victory in the U.S. Senate that spring.

One day in 1975 there was an opportunity for my brother Bob, who was between jobs. He was visiting me in Washington, D.C. I was going to meet Culver at National Airport and take him to his house. So I brought Bob along, and Culver made this point that I've always remembered. "When I finished Harvard," John said, "I had a lot friends who had all these options in front of them. Should I go down to New York and make a lot of money? Should I go back home and run my family's business? Should I run for office and be a politician? Should I be a person who goes into international affairs and do the state department or international business?"

He added, "I had friends who always wanted to keep their options open and had a hard time nailing down one of them because they never wanted to leave something else behind. That's not something that makes sense. It makes more sense to grab one of the options and try to make a success of that. Then, if that doesn't work, try something else because you'll always be able to try something else. If you keep all your options open so long that you can't really make a success of one of them, you're not going to be very happy." That was very sound advice to me and my brother.

As we went forward in April and May 1975, it appeared to me that I was looking at six more years of very time-consuming work day and night. By then Mardi and I had a baby, Allison, who was a few months old. We bought a tiny house up in northwest Washington, D.C. from one of Culver's departing staff members. I just felt that I was not going to be happy staying there for six more years, missing out on raising my daughter, and being away from my wife morning, noon, and night including weekends.

The final straw was Sen. Culver returning from a meeting of the Tri-Lateral Commission. The group included members such as former Georgia Gov. Jimmy Carter and Henry Kissinger, and leaders from two or three continents. They had a meeting one week in late spring or early June. I believe it was in Tokyo, Japan. My role was to watch over the office and relations in Iowa even though I was not in the best paid or highest profile job. I could hardly enjoy a Friday or a Saturday or a Sunday because I had to pay attention to whether Culver could get back from Tokyo, where he could land, and how he could get from the airport to his house in Maryland.

In those days we didn't have telephones that enabled you to get away from your living room so I had to stay by the phone or have Mardi stay by the phone if I went outside. I knew I could see what needs to be done, and I gladly had done that kind of work for the whole six years with Sen. Harold Hughes. But I did not look forward to six more years of that kind of responsibility.

I paid attention. Culver did fly into Baltimore late at night. I drove up and met him at the Baltimore airport. He was exhausted and a little angry at Carter and Kissinger and the way the meeting had gone. I drove him back to his house and went back home, thinking this is not what I want to do for the next six years.

That's when I opened a discussion with St. Ambrose College. I told the man who had been my high school teacher that maybe I'd be interested in coming back next year. I thought maybe I'd come back in 1976 and resume my teaching career. When I made that call, they called back the next day and said, "You can come back this summer [of 1975] if you'd like to teach in the fall."

It was news to my wife, Mardi, that this was even possible. She had thought we'd done all this. We'd gotten married. We had a baby and bought a house. It looked like I had a job for the next six years with

Culver. And all of a sudden, I dropped the idea on her that maybe I'd go back to Davenport and teach. She was surprised, but she did not object.

It was a surprise to my mother who was living alone in Davenport, too. She did not expect to see me back there. We moved back to Davenport and found a rental home near St. Luke's Hospital not far from where she lived. I taught at St. Ambrose College in 1976 and 1977. Sen. Culver kept in touch with me and invited me sometimes to go with him to events in southeast Iowa. One of his staff people asked me if I would consider coming back on the staff as a part-time consultant while continuing to teach at St. Ambrose.

I talked that over with Park Rinard who was administrative assistant in John's office. Park said, "Pat, you've taken a teaching job. You have a bunch of priests who run St. Ambrose College who know you well. You've got to make a success of that job." Then I talked to Harold Hughes, my old boss. He said almost the same thing. "Pat, what I know about politicians is they try to spread themselves too thin," Hughes said. "Get your teaching job nailed down, and then you can run for office if you want to!"

———

After we were married in 1973, Mardi and I got an apartment not far from George Washington University. Dan Miller's apartment at George Washington University was just a couple blocks away from us. Dan rode to work with me during much of 1975 while working for Sen. Culver. We worked for Culver during January, February, March, April, May, and June 1975.

One day in 1975 Dan and I walked over to an office at the U.S. Capitol called the disbursing office. In those days you could cash a check at the disbursing office. So we walked over together and cashed our checks. When we got done with that, I took an envelope out of my pocket and showed Dan. The envelope had a return address of St. Ambrose College, Davenport, Iowa.

He looked at it and said, "Are you going back there to teach?" And I said, "Yes." Dan said, "Wow!" I've talked to Dan's widow since then to get these dates straight. He immediately took steps that summer to be employed by an emerging Iowa public television network, the Iowa Educational Broadcast Network. He told me that fall when we were both back in Iowa, "You know, I'm setting up a program" that became known as *Market to Market*. Dan was the creator of *Market to Market* as early as November or December 1975.

At that point, I had been teaching for three or four months. He moved back to Iowa and negotiated this job. Dan had a great career in public broadcasting. He fashioned this program around the same things that I fashioned my political interests: the issues and the contacts in Washington and Iowa.

The story has not been told. When Dan died, the obituary did not even mention working for Culver because nobody around Dan remembered that. A comment was made at a celebration of life for Dan after his death that "you should call Pat Deluhery to get the story straight." Over the years, Dan fashioned the public affairs component of Iowa Public Television to be what it is today. At the end of his career he was the top guy at Iowa Public Television.

One of my friends in Davenport, Thom Hart, approached me that August 1975 and said, "The mayor has asked me to come and talk to you. We want you to be on the ballot this fall for city treasurer." I declined. Next year, a different guy came to me and said, "We'd like you to run for county supervisor." Once again, I declined. The next year (1977) a delegation of people came to me and said, "We want you to run for mayor in 1977 and we're not going to take 'no' for an answer."

On that one, I decided to fly out to Washington, D.C. and ask Park Rinard, "Does it make sense to run for mayor?" Park said, "No. Tell me a mayor who's run for office who's ever been very successful because hardly any one of them have." It's a terrible job in Iowa government. So I declined that invitation. And Park said, "Run for either state representative or state senator if a seat is available. If you get that, that's a good job." It was good advice.

CHAPTER 15

JUGGLING ACT

DELUHERY LEADS busy life with family, politics, and teaching position at St. Ambrose.

I resumed teaching at St. Ambrose College in 1975, teaching economics in the fall of 1975, the spring of 1976, and the summer of 1976. I also taught business administration in the fall of 1977 and the spring of 1978.

How do you manage marriage and the family along with serving in political office and being a full-time college teacher? Besides those two jobs I was a community leader. If you're a community leader, you're called on to represent the community when other people come through town or when the community needs some presence in Des Moines or Washington, D.C. I had to play that part in a very careful way because of the demands of teaching and the governmental office that I held. Careful, meaning I was scheduled tightly frequently. You cannot be in two places at once so you just have to say no to people. Because I had a wife and three children, being part of their life also was something I wanted. It's the reason I left Washington and moved back to Iowa.

The house on Rusholme Street worked fairly well because it's central to Davenport. You could go in any of four directions and practically be five minutes away from anything in the community. Frequently I'd be doing something that related to public service at eight-thirty in the morning, teaching at ten, ten-thirty, or eleven in the morning, working with students at St. Ambrose in the afternoon, going to some event at 4 o'clock or 5 o'clock that related to being a senator or a candidate for the state Senate, and yet home for dinner and possibly going out that night.

People would say, "I don't know how you manage all of this." I stayed focused in dealing with students and the demands at St. Ambrose. I could move from one subject to another relatively easily, shift gears and be on the next page later. It would have been impossible to do all that if Mardi weren't so highly competent in dealing with all other parts of our lives. In my experience in Washington, D.C. and serving in the Iowa Senate, I saw numerous families in which if one of the two parents was having a bad week, a bad month or a bad year, everything could fall apart.

In 1976, none other than Jimmy Carter, the Democratic presidential nominee, called Don O'Brien in Sioux City and said, "Don, I know how well thought of you are around the nation. We want you to leave Iowa and run the campaign in California." By then, I was a citizen in Davenport, thinking of running in 1978. Don said to me, "You know, Pat, I don't need this. I have a law practice in Sioux City. Now I have to leave everything, go out to California, and run the Carter-for-president campaign." But I understood why the Carter campaign wanted him. Frequently campaigns do the best if they bring in a good outsider who can call things in a very honest and even-handed way and in a way that politicians don't think of the person as a future rival. Yes, O'Brien went out to California and ran the campaign for Carter.

When O'Brien was back in Sioux City, the president of the United States was Jimmy Carter. And Carter nominated O'Brien to be a federal judge for the northern district of Iowa. Second, the *Des Moines Register* went on a rampage that O'Brien should not be confirmed by the U.S. Senate. The *Register* knew O'Brien and didn't think he was that good a lawyer. Then the Senate confirmed him. Culver called Sioux City one day, and when O'Brien came on the line, he said "Hello, Judge O'Brien," meaning we just confirmed you.

My sister, Sheila, had moved from Dubuque to Davenport in 1978 or 1979 with her two children, Mary and Tony Funderburk. We were a Dubuque family living in Davenport for the last twenty-five years. But we weren't as connected as people who had gone back a hundred years in Davenport who were my contemporaries. Our daughter, Norah, was born in 1977, and there were about five years difference between her and Mary. All four kids got pulled together to do all kinds of things. For example, we would drive from Davenport in one station wagon over to Iowa City to see my brother, Bob, and his wife, Camille. Bob and Camille then moved to North Liberty on the banks of Lake McBride. Norah was always striving to live up to the standards set by Mary and Allison who were quite a bit older. Norah did well at it; she has a lot going for her. She could always excel at things.

She had the lead in *The Sound of Music* in the fall of her senior year in high school. She played Maria, the caregiver who comes in and has to manage seven kids; teach them to sing; and deal with the father of the family. Norah played that role on a Friday night, a Saturday night, and a Sunday afternoon. The woman running the theater for Davenport Assumption High School did an extremely professional job of costuming, music, and dance. In that sense, it was a fitting description of Norah Deluhery as superstar.

From my perspective, Norah had always been aiming for this because her cousin Mary and sister Allison were always further ahead of her. So Norah had all that level of achievement to shoot for. We invited a bunch of people to go to the Sunday afternoon matinee and had a little gathering at our house afterward. The cast had a party at one place. There were other parties going on at other places, but Norah came back to our house for that party. I remember Mayor Thom Hart, our neighbor down the street, saying the level of professionalism of that theater for a high school performance was amazing.

As she was going into the spring semester of her senior year, I told her she could bear down and probably win some scholarships, which she did. Years later, she said some of her friends wished they had done more of that themselves. She won three or four scholarships, some of which could go to any college or others to specific colleges.

One scholarship I believe was offered by the Rural Electric Co-op. The students applying for the scholarship had to go to a specific location and write their essay under supervision. Norah did some careful preparation, thought it through, and made notes. In the end she went to the event. Somebody watched the students writing their essays. She won a $5,000 scholarship from the Light and Power Co-op to any college of her choice in America. Plus, she won a scholarship from Catholic University for being a good student.

After graduation, she got a job around the department of economics at Columbia University in New York City. After that, she decided to work in the Obama campaign in 2008 and went down to Washington, D.C. where she is today.

In the middle of the 2008 campaign, the New York Choral Society including Norah was invited to sing in a pre-Olympic festival in Beijing, China. They had 140 voices, and there was room on the planes for sixty more people. I was one of the sixty who was nominated to go. We had to pay for our own plane ticket. We were guests of the Chinese people when we got to China. We were there for maybe two weeks and it was a lot of fun. There was a typical Chinese communist approach to the event. In Beijing there was one big choral concert in a lovely hall with a crowd of guests. The choral society also was invited to sing at three or four private concerts in government buildings where some of the top people in China were in the audience. We were down in Qingdao the next week.

Then we had the option of another five days in China so Norah and I chose the group of about forty people that went up into the mountains. In the mountains of China, you are in a civilization that was five hundred or more years old. We went to a place with a market in a little village that was at the end of five or six walkways that might have gone back two hundred miles. The people walked down to this market; they set up shop there. They sold their stuff for a couple of weeks and then walked back to where they came from. From the viewpoint of a person like me who taught economics, it was pure market economics.

This is what markets looked like prior to money, newspapers, advertising, and all the rest. Each shop was only six feet across and six feet deep with a table. Then they set up a tent behind the table. There might have been two hundred tables. They sold everything including fruits and vegetables and hand goods. Everybody knew if you had something to sell and saved up for six months or a year, buyers would be there. People were there from all over the world. You'd see a young boy and girl maybe twenty-two or twenty-five years old with their backpacks. They were from Scandinavia. What were they doing backpacking in China? Well, that's what they were doing – backpacking. I talked to some people who could speak English. This was an ancient form of commerce that was five centuries old.

CHAPTER 16

'78 STATE SENATE BID

DELUHERY RUNS for political office for first time amidst turmoil of the 1970s.

As it happened, there was a state Senate seat Bill Gluba had occupied that was held by a Republican named Forrest Ashcraft at the time. So in the summer of 1977, I made a move to run in 1978 for the Senate seat. I lived in the district; we'd bought a house there. By then we had two children, Allison and baby Norah. I announced I was interested in that seat. Then I announced for the seat with a lot of help from people in the Iowa General Assembly and people in Washington, D.C., including Park. They weren't making calls on my behalf, but they guided me. They told me who to contact and who to avoid if I was thinking about running for something like a seat in the Iowa Senate.

Iowa government looked like this: Bob Ray, a Republican, was governor. All the rest of the statewide seats from lieutenant governor on down were occupied by Republicans. On the other hand, the General Assembly was dominated by Democrats who had the majority in the Senate and the House. How did that happen? It happened because of Dick Clark winning the 1972 U.S. Senate race against Jack Miller in an astounding upset. So Clark was the U.S. senator from Iowa starting in 1973. And Culver won the Senate in 1974, defeating David Stanley. With Clark and Culver's wins, widespread candidate recruitment, very good organization, the turmoil of the 1970s, the movement against the war in Vietnam, rock festivals, and young people not wanting to fold into the way the World War II generation lived, the state was in great turmoil and in flux electorally. It was in the midst of all that I decided to run for the Iowa Senate.

We spent about $12,000 in that 1978 campaign. Of that $12,000, I put $5,000 of my own money as a loan to the campaign, although it was never repaid. By the 1996 Senate campaign, I had little control over the money or the spending. My campaign committee in 1996 reported $300,000 in contributions. In addition to that, another $300,000 was spent by Democratic Party committees on my behalf that did not come through my campaign committee. So we spent $600,000 on my side. My opponent had the same numbers. They reported approximately $300,000. In addition, another $300,000 was spent on his behalf.

Who spent that extra $600,000? Two or three days after the election, I got a call from somebody I didn't know in Washington, D.C. He said, "You know, Pat, that money was raised by Al Gore." I also learned that on the other side, that $300,000 was spent by Newt Gingrich. So were Gore and Gingrich involved in a Senate race in Iowa in 1996? I'd say yes. It's not only possible, it's almost certainly true. It isn't the main thing they thought about. With $5 million to spend, they may have decided in less than thirty seconds to put some of that money into the Iowa race.

Roger Jepsen was a late contestant for the Republican nomination for the U.S. Senate in 1978. A couple of other Republican candidates were allies of Gov. Ray. Then Roger decided, maybe four or five days before the filing deadline, that he would run for the Senate. He got in so late that he barely got his papers filed with the secretary of state. The *Des Moines Register* was very hostile to Jepsen, and a lot of Gov. Ray's people didn't like him either. But he also had a certain pizzazz that was lacking on their side. He knew how to give a speech. He knew how to run a race. He had a flair to him. And his wife, Dee, was a terrific asset. She was a friend and associate of Meredith Deevers, the wife of my father's employee who had bought Deluhery Electric Co.

Roger won the Republican primary. So he was running against Dick Clark, who was enormously popular with the Iowa press. Roger was regarded as an outlier. A lot of the press treated him as though it was hard to take him seriously. But Roger was tougher than they all thought. Dick Clark was running a good campaign, so it was Clark against Jepsen for the U.S. Senate, then the House races, the governor's race, and the statewide races including my first race for the Iowa Senate. It was the first time I noticed there was a new religious element going on in politics. There was a popular church in the west end of Davenport called the West Side Assembly of God.

On the Friday before Election Day, Dick Clark was campaigning at an event in Davenport. Clark came over to me and said, "How's your campaign going?" I said, "Pretty well." Then he said, "How do you think mine is going?" And I said, "Not so good." He was surprised. He looked at me sharply. "Why do you say that?" he asked. I said, "Well, I just think you have not defined any issues that you want to run on or work on in the next six years." His answer was, "Interesting."

On the next Saturday and Sunday I was down at the Assembly of God with the Rev. Tommy Barnett. The other people campaigning there were Roger and Dee Jepsen, and Dee said hello to me. Roger came over and said, "How do you think the campaign is going?" I said, "Well, it's very close." He said, "You mean mine?" I said, "Yeah." And he said, "Really?"

The *Des Moines Register* was giving him such a hard time, but something was going on in America that was the end of the Jimmy Carter presidency two years later and the defeat of Culver and six or seven other Democratic U.S. senators two years later. Roger Jepsen defeated Dick Clark, and within a day or two of that election, the *Register* ran an editorial that said the best man lost and what a mistake the voters made.

By January 1981, Roger Jepsen was so disgruntled at the *Register* that when President Ronald Reagan came to Iowa for an event, the president gave an exclusive interview to George Mills of the AP, not the *Register*. Two or three years later there were comments by *Register* staffers acknowledging they were a little off base in the '78 Senate race by saying the best man lost.

Daughter Rose was born in 1979. I was already a one-year member of the Iowa Senate. Rose was born with a heart defect and Down Syndrome. Doctors at the University of Iowa Hospitals and Clinics told us when she was only six weeks old that she would need heart surgery. For Mardi and me, and especially Mardi, coping with Rose's health issues and her education has been a very important responsibility. It's also been a thread in Allison's and Norah's life from the time of Rose's birth to today.

Rose attended school in Davenport in special education until she was twenty-one years old. She had two successful open heart surgeries at age four and twenty-six. As an adult, she has lived a happy life with us these last twenty years.

The Republicans held the majority in 1979, my first year in the Iowa Senate. I opposed a bill calling for a constitutional convention that was supported by Iowans for Tax Relief and David Stanley. President Jimmy Carter got blamed after a snowstorm shut down Interstate 35 near the Missouri state line. Not only did Republicans blame Carter for problems on the interstate, but also they wanted to hold a constitutional convention to balance the budget. A cartoon by Pulitzer Prize-winning cartoonist Frank Miller after the snowstorm reflected my remarks on the Senate floor then. The top of the cartoon shows a man in a top hat calling for cutting federal spending, slashing all programs, balancing the budget, fighting inflation, and holding a constitutional convention. The lower part of the cartoon with the caption "What a difference some snow makes!" shows the same man buried in snow asking the federal government to send lots of money quickly for disaster relief.

During the summer of 1980, my mother-in-law, Peggy Morris, said to me, "Pat, these have been a very busy five or six years for you and Mardi. Life isn't always like this."

Of course, she was right.

During my first five years in the Iowa Senate, Mardi and our daughters moved to Des Moines with me for the Iowa General Assembly from January to the end of May. Then we'd live on Rusholme Street in Davenport for the rest of the year. That ended as the children got past the early grades in school.

Mardi was hired by the Mississippi Bend Area Education Agency (AEA) to start a new program: the Parent Educator Connection. The AEA served multiple school districts in five eastern Iowa counties. The program was designed to improve communication between the parents of children with disabilities and the special education professionals in the state's schools.

After I'd been in the Iowa Senate three or four years, Park Rinard said to me, "Elected officials don't have that many opportunities to do things together with other people." Other people our age would have a social circle they met with regularly. In fact, Mardi and I are like that today. We have people we see regularly, share meals with, and do things with. Rinard pointed out "that's one of the immense sacrifices you make when you serve in elective office." Yes, you're going to give that up if you're elected. And what do other people see? Sure, you get a lot of attention, but you also make sacrifices.

There are financial sacrifices, too. Neither the Iowa Senate nor St. Ambrose College were all that highly paid. There were lobbyists in Des Moines who made five or ten times the annual income that I made. Sometimes they'd say, "Well, you're really paying your dues," meaning you're living a lifestyle that's below what you could afford if you did some other kind of work. Arthur Small, a state senator from Iowa City, would describe why he only had a couple of suits of clothes. He'd wear one suit on Monday, Wednesday, and Friday and a different one on Tuesday, Thursday, and Saturday. He would say, "You just don't make that much money serving in the Iowa Senate with your wife working on a doctorate at Iowa City." And that's correct. To the outside world, it looks like members of Congress make this great big salary. But they don't make that much money compared with the expenses they have.

Our life became a little more predictable after 1984. During the spring legislative session, I'd drive home every weekend. After teaching in the summer session at St. Ambrose, we'd drive to New York to see Mardi's family. We managed to get the Morris family together on Cape Cod, Lake George, and the Atlantic coast in Maine. We were – and are – a happy family.

Nevertheless, other people could look at us and see our situation differently.

We were at a small gathering in Davenport one weekend. I saw a woman I barely knew talking intently to Mardi.

After a few minutes, the woman broke off the conversation, walked over, and angrily said, "Your wife is a saint!"

I did a double take. Startled, I didn't reply. Well, I thought, things look differently to different people.

Mardi became the go-to person on Rusholme Street. For many years, we had a big summer block party in front of our house. Mardi went to City Hall to get the proper permits. Barriers were delivered to the ends of Brady and Pershing streets.

With the street blocked, the kids would play and ride their bikes from noon to seven o'clock. Meanwhile, the adults would socialize and picnic. It was a big joint effort. However, it always seemed to be a wildly happy time for people who treasured family and neighbors.

Going forward to 1996, I'm in this campaign where the opposition is running $30,000 of negative television advertising against me every week for six weeks. And in the middle of all of that, Judge O'Brien decides a prisoner in the federal penitentiary system isn't being taken care of well enough over some issue involving television or something like that. So O'Brien issued an opinion on one federal prisoner. Within two or three days, the opposition was running an ad against me in Davenport that said, "Have you heard the latest? Have you heard that a judge has decided a prisoner should have a color television set?" Their approach was to get voters angry for about thirty seconds, then take another thirty seconds to attach that anger to state Sen. Pat Deluhery.

Nonetheless, I won a close race. But O'Brien himself said something to me later: "Pat, I know what happened in that campaign with my decision, but when decisions are in front of you, you have to make them." I thought to myself, "Why couldn't you have delayed your decision until after Election Day?" But it was the last thing in the world he would have thought about.

When Jim Lykam was elected to the Iowa House of Representatives in 2003, we invited him to bring his wife and son to our house on a Sunday afternoon for chili dinner. We also invited our neighbors, Mayor Thom Hart and his wife, Jane, and state Reps. Tom Fey and Bob Arnould with their wives.

It was a great afternoon. Why? Because no one was there to lobby you on issues.

I thought the wives, particularly Barb Lykam, would later encounter each other and share a laugh over some of the absurdities that accompany their spouses' election to public office.

CHAPTER 17

LANDMARK LEGISLATION

DELUHERY PLAYS major role in passage of environmental, energy legislation in Iowa.

1987, Groundwater Protection Act; 1989, Waste Volume Reduction and Recycling Act; and 1990, the Energy Efficiency Act.

I floor managed each of these above bills through the Iowa Senate. I represented the Senate in negotiations with the Iowa House to get to a finished bill. I won awards for all three bills from Washington, D.C.-based groups that singled them out for attention and recommended them to other legislators around the nation. The Washington, D.C. group was called the Center for Policy Alternatives.

Like a lot of things in my life, I had little idea of all the other things going on around me that impacted what I was doing. How did I know that the Center for Policy Alternatives was going to select that first bill, the Groundwater Protection Act, for its Best Bet Award? But it did.

In 1987 our governor was Terry Branstad. He had been elected governor in 1982 when Gov. Robert Ray left office voluntarily. When Branstad was elected governor in 1982, both houses of the General Assembly had flipped from Republican control to Democratic control. So as we took office in 1983, which was the beginning of my second term, Democrats were in the majority in the Senate until 1996.

The approach in the 1987 bill endured for me before and after 1987. The approach was that both the House and Senate of the General Assembly would have an interim study committee in the fall before we convened in January 1987. At the time, I was teaching economics at St. Ambrose, but I taught summer school for six weeks and I taught the fall semester, which began at the end of August and finished before Christmas. St. Ambrose allowed me to teach on a Tuesday-Thursday schedule with no classes on Friday. This gave me Fridays to come to Des Moines in the fall for an interim study committee meeting.

The Senate majority leader named me as the chair of the interim study committee for the Senate. Then I would have a chair from the House, and the two of us would run the interim study committee. The Senate majority leader at the time was Bill Hutchins from just west of Des Moines, a rural and small town in Iowa. At the time, I was vice chair of the Commerce Committee and chair of the Environment Committee.

We scheduled these interim study committee meetings on a Friday. Typically, we'd have one at the end of September, one in October, and maybe one in November or early December. In each case, I had already worked through issues in the U.S. Senate and the Iowa Senate, so I knew how to approach issues with expert staff and three or four different contacts around the statehouse and around the state.

I would always emphasize to the speakers we scheduled for these interim study committees that we wanted them to describe the problem. Do not try to sell us on your solution, I told them. Just tell us what is the problem. So we would have a meeting organized by staff in Des Moines in which we would have a panel of speakers. The meetings typically would be at 10 a.m. til noon or 12:30 p.m. and then from 1 or 1:30 p.m. til three-thirty in the afternoon.

The problem on the groundwater bill involved farm chemicals sold to kill weeds and unwelcome vegetation. They would flow from the farm fields right into the ground and creeks, finding their way into the groundwater of Iowa. The farm chemical residue would show up in the drinking water of Iowa families. The agricultural community in Iowa resisted this description of the problem. First, they would say, "Don't blame us, blame the lawn care industry." It was correct. Around the state the lawn care industry was a major source of groundwater pollution. The farm community would also call this "modern agriculture." Modern agriculture involved the use of chemicals.

Both Don Avenson, the speaker of the House, and Hutchins, the majority leader of the Senate, wanted to get a bill passed. They accommodated me and the House members of the interim study committee by giving us the go-ahead to frame the issue and describe for the press what was going on with the issue. There was an enormous amount of press attention on the issue. In those days the *Des Moines Register*, the Associated Press, and the big newspapers in the urban centers around Iowa – Davenport, Cedar Rapids, Waterloo, Mason City, Sioux City, Fort Dodge, and Council Bluffs – picked up on these issues in a very big way. It filled the gap for them on what the state might be working on the next January when the General Assembly convened. All interim study committee meetings were widely covered by statewide press.

U.S. Sen. Paul Simon of Illinois had a background in the world of journalism. Simon had once been a state legislator and he married a state legislator, so his wife was a former state representative like him. The Illinois Quad Cities and Iowa Quad Cities labor leaders in 1986 and 1987 liked Simon. They knew him. And I liked Simon because I liked his approach. I was quite prepared to support him for president. On the Illinois side of the Quad Cities there was a big Labor Day celebration, so I had been introduced to Simon.

In the spring of 1987 we were working on the Groundwater Protection Act. Simon was in Iowa looking to gather support for his 1988 bid for president, and my picture appeared in the *Des Moines Register* three times in one week over the groundwater protection bill. It was humorous because here's Simon running for president trying to get some attention in the *Des Moines Register* and here's Deluhery who Simon knew and might be supporting Simon's candidacy, getting all this attention in the *Des Moines Register*. He commented on it to me: "You really do well over groundwater protection." He laughed.

We created a center at Iowa State University that relates to agriculture and keeping agriculture abreast of issues that are related to groundwater and the environment. Two or three years into the center, the center asked me if I would be willing to write an introduction for its annual report. I really worked on that introduction for the annual report. The introduction had a phrase that I wrote that set a standard and explained the 1987 Groundwater Protection Act.

The introduction of my few paragraphs was as follows: "Mothers and grandmothers led to the passage of the 1987 Groundwater Protection Act. Their concerns over their children and grandchildren led the farm lobby to relent on their opposition to passing some kind of a bill. When they relented, we could then fold in protections in regard to the urban side of this issue, which is the grass cutting, lawn care, and weed elimination industry, which was a very big industry at the time."

1989: The Waste Volume Reduction and Recycling Act

Once again, the Democrats were in control of the Senate and the House. The governor was Terry Branstad, a Republican. The press attention to these issues was immense. We used the same approach. I chaired an interim study committee along with the House chairman of the interim study committee. We had meetings all fall on Fridays.

To describe the issue briefly, landfills are a very expensive way to deal with garbage and trash. The federal laws were changing and they were requiring landfills to be much more carefully protected, meaning you had to lay down some kind of a cover that kept what was in the landfill from draining into the nearby creeks. The cover was an industrial-scale blanket underneath the trash.

At the time people would cut their grass and put their leaves and grass in plastic bags, put the plastic bags into the garbage can, and take the garbage and toss it into this very costly landfill. There were people who could describe how expensive every square foot and every cubic foot in the landfill was to get established. It was exorbitant. To have a cubic foot of trash in a landfill, you were putting this very pricey cover underneath it, and preparing for a very expensive burial of trash. In short, it was ridiculous to put grass clippings in a plastic bag and bury it in a landfill.

It was worse out in the rural areas. I served with some farmers in the General Assembly. I can remember a guy named Gene Fraise from Fort Madison, Iowa, a very good legislator. Fraise would describe how on say, a 160- or 320-acre farm, there was an area that was not particularly tillable. It would be where there was a ditch or an indentation. You'd find old vehicles, cars, tractors, and machinery left over from fifty and sixty years earlier in these ditches. When the equipment was worn out, the farmers would simply push it into the ravine and just let it sit there.

Needless to say, from the viewpoint of the sophisticated scientists at Iowa State University and the University of Iowa, all of this looked as ridiculous as it sounds today thirty years later. But in the world of 1989, that's the way life was lived in the Midwest and no doubt in other places around the nation.

I taught economics for years. I would say to the students: "You can get confused about all the things that are going on in economics, so just try to focus on two or three goals. One is growth of the gross domestic product. A second is price stability; that is, try to maintain no inflation, and then go to two or three different policy instruments: monetary policy and fiscal policy. The third goal is full employment. You want employment to be full, the gross domestic product (GDP) to increase, and prices to remain stable.

The prevailing wisdom in the '80s was that everything you dump in the landfill is not an addition to gross domestic product. Our measurements were all wrong. It wasn't that the measurements weren't useful; it was that we weren't figuring out how to recycle things or use things differently in our measurement of GDP and price stability. I learned in 1963 and 1964 at Notre Dame and for three years at the London School of Economics that it takes stepping back and looking at it in a different way.

What we wanted to do was a critique. I gave Lady Bird Johnson credit from 1963 to 1968 when I was studying and teaching economics. She would point out that if you drive around America into any big city, you drive by a great big automobile dump on the edge of town on open land, where there will be up to a thousand junked automobiles. The junked automobiles are brought to these places where the private sector will assemble them and use them for money-making activities. Lady Bird's message was Beautify America – let's get these junked autos out of sight of the entrances to every one of our big cities in America.

In my family, my father and mother strongly endorsed that viewpoint. Lady Bird was onto something. We don't need to have an automobile graveyard sitting on empty land right at the edge of all our cities. Get 'em out of here. Do something with them. There is value in all that steel. There's value in other parts. Let's do something that gives incentive to industry to move the automobiles out of sight and break them down more promptly. From my perspective, that relates to a family in the Quad Cities. They had industrial sites along the Mississippi River. They were very familiar with shipping up and down the Mississippi River. My father did a lot of electrical work for them. One of them was named Joman Steel. The first name was made out of the first names of a couple of the owners – Joe and Herman. Another would be Harry Alter & Sons.

There's money to be made in picking up what people think of as trash and doing something imaginative with it. That is, pull out the constituent parts and develop them into some other use. A few years after the 1989 bill, a plant was established west of Bluegrass, Iowa close to the Scott County line. I played a role in this plant coming to the Quad Cities. The IPSCO plant accumulated junked cars and other final products that had steel components. They were brought to this plant and broken down, and the constituent parts went into the American industrial marketplace.

The plant is one of three that exist in North America. The earliest of the three plants was just across the line in Canada. The third plant is downriver two or three states south of Iowa. All three plants were recycling plants in modern terms. I helped facilitate the deal they wanted through Iowa state government and the General Assembly.

When IPSCO decided to build this recycling plant near Bluegrass, a Davenport supporter, Jack Bush, whose wife was a McCarthy, said to me, "Pat, this is the biggest deal we've ever been involved in in the history of the [quarry] company." Why was that? They had to stabilize the location by bringing rock from McCarthy's Davenport quarries and laying it down so you'd have a stable base. Truckload after truckload of rock – no doubt numbering in the hundreds – were carried from nearby Buffalo, Iowa to the IPSCO plant site. Then topsoil was put on the rock before the plant was built. That was a big thing in the history of the Quad Cities.

1990: The Energy Efficiency Act

So now we're in 1990. What is the problem to be addressed? We continued to have very good relations between the majority leader of the Iowa Senate and the speaker of the Iowa House. Don Avenson in the House was planning a run for governor in 1990. Bill Hutchins was still the majority leader in the Iowa Senate. I was playing a key role in two or three committees that could have jurisdiction in this. So the 1989 interim study committee had to look at how our utility companies were functioning and try to pass a bill that gave the companies more incentive to do energy efficiency as opposed to building more electrical generating plants. The Iowa Commerce Commission was the regulator.

Here was the problem: The incentives for the electric and gas utilities were set to reward them for using more electricity and charging more for it rather than selling their client base on using electricity in a more sensible way. How can you attempt to turn those incentives around? Turning those incentives around meant giving the electric utilities incentives to try to sell their customers on energy efficiency, using energy more sensibly, and allowing the utilities to collect for doing that. In this way, the building of more expensive electrical generating plants is forestalled.

And that's what we were really aiming for – to defer the building of more expensive power plants. There also was a big discussion of whether we should use nuclear because nuclear plants already existed in Cedar Rapids and the Quad Cities on the Illinois side. The companies in this discussion included Iowa-Illinois Gas & Electric, later known as MidAmerican Energy. MidAmerican Energy became something of a conglomerate, and today it's owned by Warren Buffett, the billionaire investor from Omaha, Nebraska.

The problem to be addressed was that the utility companies had every incentive for their customers to use more electricity and every incentive to build more plants and no incentive to try to show their customers how to be more efficient in their energy usage. It seems simple enough to describe today in 2020, but at the time it was wildly controversial. My friend and supporter, Dick Kautz, said to me at the time that the chairman of the board of Iowa-Illinois Gas & Electric got on his nerves and shook him up by saying, "Pat Deluhery is a socialist." They were in a mind-set that their job was to make money by selling electricity.

I had two or three contacts inside that company. My father had worked closely with them since the 1950s. In almost every electrical job you do, you're dealing with the power company. The electrical contractor's job is to wire a plant or a building and coordinate with the electric utility at the point where they bring the energy in to hook up that energy to the new project. The contractor and the electric utility have to coordinate to create a usable energy source. If it were water, it would be like reducing a flow in gallons to a flow in quarts or even pints. Or, if the power is already reduced, they try to make it come in in the most efficient way possible, doing the least amount of damage to the appearance or efficiency of the project. It also has to be easy for the power company to monitor the meters to see how much power has been used.

There was an issue in a 1950s job, the brand-new television station building that served the biggest channel in Davenport, Channel 6 radio and TV. Deluhery Electric wired a brand-new facility there more or less on the grounds of Palmer College of Chiropractic. The name of the electrician who ran the job was Patch. My father really liked Patch. My father said to me one time, "Patch had the ideal job. He would start the job and take the job all the way to the end over a couple-of-years period."

Between the contractor and the gas and electric company and everybody else involved, they brought the power in from the north side of the job to this TV station, which has a very nice front entrance that looks at Brady Street in Davenport. The power was coming in from behind, and my father's point was "we should have spent the money to bore down all the way to the ground level and then bring the power in there."

Instead of that, they brought the power in one or two floors up because the station was being built on the Brady Street hill. So you're coming in from the back side of the building and bringing the power in from the hill. It caused the building to rattle in the most minute way, almost truly undetectable to the human touch. But rattle it did. In today's world, it would be like an air conditioner coming on and putting your hand against the wall and feeling when the air conditioner comes on. A TV station with cameras didn't want the ground and the floors to rattle.

The owner of the company was David Palmer, a longtime associate of my dad. Palmer was incensed by this and other parts of the job because he thought, "Why didn't you guys think of this; I'm building a TV station, and I expect this to be anticipated." It was not anticipated, and there would be very expensive remedies to try to eliminate the vibration.

John Daniel, like many of these people at Iowa-Illinois Gas & Electric, was trained as an engineer. He was a great big, tall fellow. Daniel's wife was Rita Takos Daniel. Rita Takos had grown up in a family on a farm kitty-corner from the Donovan farm in Bernard. When I was a little boy, I knew her brothers, Francis and Earl. Later on as I was growing up in Davenport, I knew Rita and her sisters. Two of her sisters were nuns at Marycrest College. Rita's children were very high-profile kids in Davenport.

Here is how Iowa-Illinois Gas & Electric got started. When they were being formed in the 1940s or the early 1950s, they engaged in cutthroat pricing. Cutthroat pricing means they would identify a category of customers by neighborhood or location and then undercut the electrical rates being charged by some local company. Their goal was to put that company out of business and acquire that neighborhood as a customer.

I had people who had worked on this issue explain it to me. There was a very old agency in state government called the Iowa Commerce Commission. It had gone way back into the nineteenth century. Harold Hughes was elected to and then chair of the Iowa Commerce Commission. He served on the commission from 1958 to 1962. The role of the Commerce Commission didn't relate so much to electricity but to a lot of other things going back to the nineteenth century such as railroads, water, and all kinds of utility issues. When they brought them in, it was to prevent companies like Iowa-Illinois Gas & Electric from killing their local competition.

The name of that chairman of the board of Iowa-Illinois Gas & Electric was Charley Whitmore. Even in high school, I heard him described as a brilliant businessman. He was assembling a gas and electric company that was becoming a prominent player in the Davenport-Rock Island marketplace.

Another feature of that company that is relevant to our story is when Alcoa decided to build a plant upriver from Davenport, Whitmore undoubtedly was a player in that decision. Iowa-Illinois Gas & Electric put an electrical generating plant just upriver, practically adjacent to the Alcoa plant. If you go there today, you'll find that both of the plants are operating. Not only have I been in the Alcoa plant, but I've also had tours of the power plant.

Both my father and I had this viewpoint: The techniques change, but the infrastructure is not moved. It would be like a house that has central air conditioning vs. a house ten years earlier that used devices that sat in the windowsill. The same thing happened in regard to the electrical generating plant upriver from Alcoa, whose basic job was to roll out these aluminum ingots into long sheets. The power plant plays into that in a very big way.

Twenty years later, the electrical generating plant used some of the Alcoa plant's product in generating electricity, like the steam. So it was that interplay that led to me managing the 1990 energy efficiency bill.

We did give the electricity companies incentives to figure out how to get their customers to use electricity more efficiently, and they responded to that. So they figured out ways for homeowners to use energy-efficient windows, insulation, etc. We gave them a role in encouraging their customers to use energy more efficiently and get rewarded and develop expertise inside the company that led to industrial, residential, and rural customers' energy efficiency.

———

In 1983 I started my second term in the Iowa Senate. We were in a new majority in the Iowa Senate. Gov. Branstad was new. The Senate Democrats were in the majority. The House Democrats held the majority, which they maintained for ten years. They lost out in 1993, which relates to other things that were going on in America. The Democrats maintained the majority in the Senate until 1997. My associate on the House side in 1983 was Ned Chiodo. Chiodo came from Des Moines and had a political story that went way, way back to the 1940s.

My associate in the Senate was Dale Tieden, a rural legislator from northeast Iowa. Tieden knew the governor well and knew the neighborhoods where the Deluhery and Donovan families came from. His district was north of Dubuque by a couple of counties. So I had to work with Chiodo, my Democratic counterpart in the House, and Tieden, a Republican in the minority who was connected to Branstad, our newly-elected governor. Another player for me was George Kinley, a Des Moines Democrat who previously had been the majority leader in the Senate prior to my election. I got along fine with George, who was named the chair of the Commerce Committee. I was vice chair of the Commerce Committee.

George appointed me chair of a utility subcommittee for the Senate Commerce Committee. George was a major player in Iowa in the 1970s and early1980s. He was a golf pro who lived in Des Moines, had a golf shop, and knew how to play golf very well. He was a big figure in the Des Moines area. This was my fifth year in the Senate, and by then I had learned how to be a state senator and how to do a bill.

———

So what was the issue to be addressed with the 1983 utility bill? The issue was pancaking. The way utility law was set up in 1983 and the decade prior to that, the utility companies had an incentive to keep filing for new rate increases. So the gas and electric companies would file a request to the utility board, the Iowa Commerce Commission, to raise their rates on a temporary basis. Then the utility board slowly moved along considering the proposed rate increase.

In the meantime, a year would go by and the utility companies would file another request and they would get another temporary rate increase on top of their earlier one. That would be called pancaking, as in a stack of pancakes sitting on a plate. By all accounts, a few months would go by and the utility companies would file a third rate increase request. This was in the context that the Republicans had been in the governor's office all the way back to the 1968 campaign. The Commerce Commission that ruled on the companies' requests was dominated by appointees of Govs. Robert Ray and Terry Branstad. The Commerce Commission would grant the companies these temporary increases and one after another they'd pancake the increases on each other.

Finally, the commission would rule on the earliest one, and they might rule against the companies. But in the meantime, the companies were collecting a temporary increase from the second rate increase request. The companies theoretically would have to do a refund; in the meantime, the companies would file for a fourth rate increase and be given an opportunity to pancake on rate increase No. 3. So it was a system related to electricity rates related to the profitability of the gas and electric companies.

The players on the Commerce Commission in a sense were big-time politicians who had been appointed to the job because they were allies of Gov. Ray and then Gov. Branstad. It was a very old, three-person commission that Hughes had served on.

As we opened in 1983, we were given the challenge to deal with this pancake issue. Our majority leader at that time was Lowell Junkins of southeast Iowa. He was the incoming minority leader in 1979 and had given me the opportunity to deal with these issues by putting me on the Commerce Committee. The idea was to pass a bill that could force the companies and the Commerce Commission to deal with these issues promptly. While the governor appointed the commissioners and while they had a staff, the Commerce Commission was paid for by levies on the utility companies.

In other words, the Commerce Commission's budget, while it was under the control of the governor and General Assembly, was being paid for by the companies. There was something a little unfair about that because every time there were crises in state budgeting, the Commerce Committee had to take its hits along with everybody else even though it wasn't doing the taxpayers any good at all. They had their staff reduced. The whole thing was a little upside down.

So I go to a phrase that's around today: "More government, bad. Lower taxes, good." The bill got enormous attention all spring. There was a lot going on. It was Branstad's first year as governor; it was our first year in the majority. In a sense, I was much more imaginative on the Senate side – even though it was a House file with a Senate amendment – in drawing on experts who worked on the utility board and in the academic world. Toward the end of the session in the spring of 1983, we were able to pass a major amendment to the House file that reduced the incentives for pancaking with a lot of changes in how utility law was governed in Iowa.

But unbeknownst to me, an advocate on the consumer side, a very brilliant thinker and tactician, was trying to get Gov. Branstad to appoint him to the utilities board. He also had an ally at the *Des Moines Register*, a woman columnist who was a potential Pulitzer Prize winner. At first, they thought the amendment was going to be a giveaway to the companies.

But then they turned around and thought it was going to be a major improvement to the bill in that it would bring an end to pancaking and move the process forward. As the session was coming to an end, we passed the bill, the House accepted the Senate amendment, and we passed the bill again. So a major rewrite of Iowa utility law happened at the end of the 1983 legislative session.

Then the *Des Moines Register* did a major editorial about what an enormous accomplishment this was. As they came to the end of the editorial, they said, "And thanks goes to Ned Chiodo for his work on this bill." As I was reading the editorial and got to the end, I thought, "Well, I tried." I blame it on the advocate who I mentioned and the editorial writer.

A couple of lobbyists who had public interest clients immediately approached David Yepsen, who oversaw the *Register's* statehouse coverage. These lobbyists jumped all over Yepsen. They asked, "How could your editorial describe in such glowing terms what is essentially a Senate amendment to a House file and give credit to the House chairman and eliminate Deluhery?"

There's nothing to say about it other than it happened. Then Yepsen called me the first week or two after the session ended and said, "I can see that our editorial missed the mark." Essentially, he said that "we owe you one" or words to that effect. He added, "I'm going to be calling you in a few days to see what issues you think we need to address as we go into the next couple of sessions."

Within a week or two, Yepsen did a column. It included things an up-and-coming legislator thinks we'll need to address, and it featured a picture of me. My brother, Bob, was then in Iowa City, and he told me that column meant a lot to him in the sense that they don't do this for just any legislator. Today, I'd have a hard time saying what issues I raised, but I'm not exaggerating that it did happen and my picture was in the paper. It totally resulted from the fact that the *Register* had given Chiodo credit for my bill.

The person from the advocacy group who was partly responsible for this said to me that summer, "You may be upset about the *Register* doing that, but Ned Chiodo is Italian. So you shouldn't feel bad," meaning most people outside of Des Moines probably didn't read the editorial. That's what he said.

When the woman who wrote the editorial left the *Register*, it got a lot of attention. She's been a player nationwide in the world of journalism ever since. She's probably retired now, but every once in a while she shows up in Iowa because she had a lot of friends in Iowa. I learned from Park Rinard to have a light touch with the press; they don't like being bullied.

Co-author's note: The predecessor to today's Iowa Utilities Board, the Iowa Board of Railroad Commissioners, was established in 1878 with three members who regulated railroad passenger and freight rates and operations. In 1911, the Office of Commerce Counsel was formed. The agency was renamed the Iowa State Commerce Commission in 1937. In 1963, Commerce Commission terms were extended from two to six years and the positions became appointed rather than elected. The Office of Consumer Advocate was established in 1983 to represent the public interest in rate cases. In addition, the Office of General

Counsel was created to provide legal support to the commission. In 1986, the Iowa State Commerce Commission was renamed the Iowa Utilities Board. On January 18, 2011, the Iowa Utilities Board and Office of Consumer Advocate moved into a 44,460-square-foot, energy-efficient office building at 1375 E. Court Ave. in Des Moines.

Co-author's note: At least one person has observed that Pat's legislative successes concerning groundwater protection, waste volume reduction and recycling, and energy efficiency affect Iowans every time they recycle a bag of lawn clippings or turn on the lights. With climate change accelerating and Iowa's water still struggling with excess nitrates, Pat's work is more important than ever.

CHAPTER 18

19TH CENTURY IOWA BECOMES 20TH CENTURY IOWA

IOWA IS SLOW to react to 1962 Supreme Court reapportionment decision, end of prohibition.

The Baker vs. Carr decision was a 1962 U.S. Supreme Court decision that applied to the state of Tennessee. After that court case and two or three more, state legislatures and general assemblies across the nation had to be apportioned according to population. That is, if there are two state representatives, you can't have one representative or a member of Congress in a given state representing 100,000 people and another representing 400,000 people.

There had been unsuccessful efforts for years to get correct apportionment for residents of cities and municipal areas. That's illustrated right here in Iowa by a major initiative by Gov. Herschel Loveless.

If state legislatures around the nation will not address pressing, important issues, then what happens? What happens is President Franklin D. Roosevelt and the New Deal and probably lots of other things where the federal government stepped in and took over things that people might have thought states would do on their own.

After 1962 it took Iowa the best part of the 1960s to properly figure out a way to get legislative apportionment. Finally by 1970 or 1972, Iowa had a system that more or less worked. And then what?

In Iowa the last proper apportionment had been in 1901. In other words, from 1901 to 1962 the Iowa General Assembly consisted of ninety-nine counties, each with a state representative. Over the years they would add a representative or two to some of the bigger counties so that by 1962, there were something like 132 state representatives. And it was comparable in the state Senate.

From 1901 to 1962 the General Assembly worked on issues that applied to rural Iowa and maybe some other things. Generally speaking, an awful lot of urban issues were not addressed.

For instance, take the fence-viewer law. The fence-viewer law says that if you have forty acres that adjoins my forty acres, I'm required to fence from the right-hand corner of my forty acres midway to a point, and then you're required to fence from the right hand of your forty acres to the same point. My fence has to work well enough to keep my cattle out of your fields, and your fence has to work well enough to keep your cattle out of my fields, etc.

If we can't agree on the distance of the fence or whether it's adequate, then you call on a board at the county level called the "fence viewers." Then a three-person board comes out, looks at the property, and orders one or the other or both to do what they're supposed to do. If anybody refuses to do what they're supposed to do, the fence viewers can have it done by the county and charge it to you on your property taxes.

I know it's a comical illustration, but to the people involved it's very serious. When I got to the Iowa Legislature as a state senator in 1979, I heard about it from senators and House members who had served going back twenty or twenty-five years. They could describe what it was like to be a legislator before the 1962 Supreme Court decision. They argued about those kinds of things. In the meantime, the whole twentieth century had occurred.

On the other hand, the state of Iowa in the late nineteenth and early twentieth centuries had built four mental health institutes around the state, including one in Independence, Iowa, which is in northeast Iowa. We had relatives who worked at the Mental Health Institute in Independence. The state had two big facilities for children with disabilities; one at Woodward near Des Moines, and one in Glenwood in southwest Iowa. The state had other things that dated back to the Civil War such as the Annie Wittenmyer home in Davenport. So my description of the fence-viewer law can be a little exaggerated in terms of how the state could address modern issues.

But the state would not address urbanization. The children on the farms couldn't all stay on the farms, so they moved to town. The cities were growing. The population of Iowa was disbursed, not only in rural areas but also in cities. We had a lot of cities, bigger ones and smaller ones. And their interests were largely ignored at the state Legislature. That was true all around the nation, in my opinion.

Herschel Loveless was elected governor in 1956 and in 1958, and he had to battle a malapportioned, very resistant General Assembly. He convened a panel with citizens from around the state to try to come up with a way to apportion the Iowa General Assembly in a fairer way. Their report in early 1959 before the Baker vs. Carr Supreme Court decision came up with a plan that made the Iowa House of Representatives more fairly apportioned and left the Senate to be governed more by county lines. Several of the commissioners were people I knew when I worked for Sen. Harold Hughes. I even served with some of them in the Iowa Senate.

The panel's recommendation was not adopted by the General Assembly. I was invited to go to Hawkeye Boys State, which was a statewide gathering with a couple of boys from each high school. I participated in Hawkeye Boys State in 1959 in the summer before my senior year of high school. Loveless spoke to Hawkeye Boys State; I saw him there that day. He talked about trying to get fair apportionment of the Legislature. In the 1960s and 1970s when I lived in Washington, D.C., Loveless had been appointed to a federal job by President John F. Kennedy and was a member of the Washington team of former officials who had one job or another. I knew him well, and he and his wife came to our wedding in 1973.

The General Assembly met every two years for about ninety to one hundred days. The timetable had been laid out to get back home to get the planting done. Generally, the state was run by the executive branch for the remaining year and a half.

Coming from a family from Dubuque that had moved to Davenport, I was only dimly aware of the apportionment issue. In 1958-59 I was in my junior year of high school. One of our neighbors was named Garrity. I had known the Garrity family since I was in first grade. They had older boys than me; they had a younger daughter than me. At that point, they lived not far from St. Ambrose College.

Mrs. Garrity was an activist on the subject of reapportionment. Reapportionment means apportioning the House of Representatives around the nation comparable to the populations so that as one state gets bigger, it gets more representation in Congress. If another state stays the same or gets smaller in population, it gets less representation in the House of Representatives.

The law called for a census every ten years and the reapportionment of Congress. And that did happen. But it did not happen at the state level. We went through the 1930s, '40s, and '50s with the Iowa General Assembly apportioned as if it were still 1920. Some would say, in reply, you're exaggerating. On occasion a second state Senate district would be added to a county. Scott County, where I lived, had two state senators by 1962. Occasionally, some counties would be combined into a House or Senate district. The result of the failure to reapport meant that state government wasn't responsive to the typical kinds of things governments deal with for a burgeoning population.

What was America really like from 1901 to 1962? Roosevelt and the New Deal filled the gap that was left vacant by state governments around the nation that simply ignored the issues.

What was the country really like? My illustration is Prohibition. Why Prohibition? It illustrates responses to perceived needs. Prohibition has been written up in a big way in the last couple of years as being in tandem with women being allowed to vote. Both movements were led by women who thought they should be allowed to vote, which did not happen until after World War I, and who thought liquor, alcoholic beverages, and public drunkenness was a national scandal. World War I got the U.S. off dead center on both of those issues. Prohibition came to an end in the early 1930s with the election of Roosevelt in 1932.

But here in Iowa, the impulse toward prohibition remained strong from 1932 to the election of Hughes in 1962. A Des Moines area restaurant/bar illustrates the point. I went to the restaurant/bar when I first came to Des Moines and worked for Hughes in the 1968 Senate campaign. I was taken there by John Chrystal, who was state superintendent of banking at the time; he took me there after the 1968 election and in early 1969. The restaurant/bar sold wine, which theoretically was made from grapes grown on the owner's own farm in southern Iowa.

Actually, it was very good wine brought in from Italy, delivered to his farm in small casks, rebottled, and brought up to his restaurant/bar. Chrystal was an officer of the state of Iowa. My point is that many of these laws related to alcoholic beverages were routinely ignored. The restaurant/bar was very popular with legislators and lobbyists. In fact, the owner had his own exception written into the Iowa Code that allowed his and maybe a few other restaurants to sell their own wine if they grew their own grapes.

After the sale of liquor in bottles was authorized when Prohibition ended, Iowa set up this ridiculous liquor authority at the state level. Theoretically, all the liquor sold in Iowa had to be delivered first to the state liquor warehouse, and from there parceled out to the state liquor stores and taverns.

From my perspective growing up in Davenport, that was a farce. It was a farce because in Cedar Rapids the state liquor store sold three bottles of liquor for every one bottle of liquor sold in Davenport. The two counties are about the same size in population. Theoretically, Davenport would sell about the same number of bottles per person as you would sell in Cedar Rapids, not one third. Where were the other two-thirds being bought? Across the river in Illinois! There was widespread carrying of alcoholic beverages across the Mississippi River for sale in the bars and for private use. It was against the law to bring more than two bottles across the river on any one trip.

So every once in a while, the state liquor authority would dispatch highway patrol undercover to watch who bought liquor by the case in the Rock Island, Illinois liquor stores. Then the highway patrol would capture them as they came across the bridge and charge them with crimes. It would be publicized and fines would be assessed. It was one of those situations where a lack of respect for the law leads to a lack of respect for law enforcement.

My father would buy a couple of cases of alcoholic beverages at the state liquor store in Davenport in December to distribute to clients and other friends of the company. Sometimes I'd accompany him as he dropped off the bottles with people in various companies he did business with. From my father's perspective, it was sort of a Christmas present that they liked, and it was just part of doing business in the 1950s. You could hand it all out, and they were grateful.

My last example is Templeton Rye. There is a little town in Carroll County, Iowa called Templeton. It was well known among certain people that Templeton Rye, which was a bottled and branded illegal alcoholic beverage, was a favorite drink of the Chicago gangster Al Capone. So there was a regular route from Templeton down to Des Moines. Families would take the illegal beverage in the '30s and move it all the way to Chicago. Again, it was one of those things that led to a lack of respect for the law when Templeton was known as a place that made a very good rye whiskey illegally. I heard about Templeton Rye when I joined the Hughes campaign in 1968. Templeton is not far from the Garst farm. The point is, legislators came to Des Moines in the 1950s, and they'd vote dry and drink wet.

One version of Roosevelt's New Deal from 1932 to his death in 1945 was that in the 1930s Roosevelt had a very key adviser named Harry Hopkins who was from Iowa. Hopkins was a graduate of Grinnell College. Hopkins was one of the key lieutenants inside the White House close to Roosevelt. He fostered such breathtaking laws as the Social Security Act. He also must have had a hand in repealing Prohibition because that's one of the first things the Roosevelt administration did. When the administration did the New Deal programs in Iowa, one of the people who worked on the programs in Iowa was the artist Grant Wood. There also were people who worked with Wood on the New Deal programs and art colonies who lived in Davenport and were constituents of mine when I ran for the state Senate in 1978.

Then there is my friend, Jim Leach, who represented Davenport and southeast Iowa for thirty years in congress. His grandfather on his mother's side was named J.A. Smith, and Jim's name, J.A.S. Leach, refers back to that grandfather. J.A. Smith headed the New Deal programs in Iowa, starting in 1933. Wood was employed in a sense by the program that Jim's grandfather was the head of in Iowa. Going back to President Lincoln, someone from Iowa has represented the Midwest on the national scene.

So Loveless was governor of Iowa from 1956 to 1960. Then there was a Republican governor, Norman Erbe, from 1960 to 1962. Hughes was elected governor in November 1962 after the Supreme Court decision in March 1962. But the General Assembly in Iowa was not affected by that, although Hughes immediately crashed down on the liquor laws by saying, "If you're going to have these liquor laws, we're going to enforce them."

And that was the start of Iowa allowing liquor by the drink in restaurants and taverns, although not on Sunday. The business forces that work on the Republican side of the General Assembly said, "Well, if you're going to enforce the liquor laws, we'll change them." And they did, almost immediately. You could go into a restaurant or tavern and buy an alcoholic beverage. Before then, you could not.

As a recovering alcoholic, Hughes spoke with authority on the issue. When Hughes got to the U.S. Senate in 1969, Sen. Mike Mansfield, the majority leader, rather promptly named Hughes chairman of the new subcommittee on alcoholism and narcotics. Hughes got an enormous amount done on the subject as a U.S. senator almost immediately. It can be viewed in several ways. It can be viewed as irony, in that it takes one to know one. Or it can be viewed as taking action against laws that are ignored, not enforced, and bring into disrepute the whole legal system.

This same issue has played out in other ways in Iowa. It has to do with bingo and gambling. For example, in approximately 1966 at the beginning of Hughes' third term as governor, Iowa elected an attorney general, Richard Turner, who came from western Iowa. Turner, a

Republican, played to the themes of "we have laws against illegal gambling, we have laws against bingo parlors that pay cash prizes, and if we have these laws, we're going to enforce them." Turner didn't want to change the laws. He was using the same message that Hughes had earlier: "If we're going to have liquor laws, we're going to enforce them."

Until his defeat by Tom Miller in 1978, Turner always played a statewide role in playing to the constituency that was opposed to gambling, bingo parties, and churches, schools, and parent-teacher organizations using gambling as a way to raise revenues. Sometimes he staged dramatic raids that were well publicized afterward, which led to his popularity with a certain portion of the electorate.

In Davenport sometime after the 1966 election and before Turner lost to Miller in 1978, the attorney general raided a big bingo game on the second floor of a place that would have been in a typical downtown setting in Davenport. He arrested several elderly women past sixty-five years old. Of course, there was a lot of press about it. One woman he arrested would be called an "inmate of a disorderly house," and her comment to the Davenport newspaper was, "You know, to be charged as an inmate of a disorderly house at my age is something of a compliment!"

Turner had also raided a big church social with an enormous amount of gambling on the banks of the Mississippi River north of Dubuque. People watching for the incoming agents got word that they were on their way – they were only twenty miles away. So the church social took all the roulette tables and other evidence of gambling and put it on a boat. The boat was sailed offshore so that when the agents got there with Turner, he couldn't do anything because all the evidence was on a boat out in the Mississippi River.

The constituency that thought laws against gambling should be enforced applauded Turner. Yet, one constituency thought it was ridiculous. When Turner lost in the 1978 election to Miller, the Democrat running against him, the Democrats had been in charge of both houses of the General Assembly from 1974 to 1978. Turner had been made into something of a laughingstock, which relates to my general picture of the population gathering in the cities and becoming less tolerant of these religious-oriented, small town, and rural Iowa laws and law enforcement. In a sense, we were moving on to a new Iowa. The election of Hughes in 1962 and Republican Bob Ray in 1968 as governor was a signal that the state was much more twentieth century than it was late-nineteenth century.

When Hughes was elected again in 1964 as governor, Lyndon Johnson carried Iowa over Republican Barry Goldwater for president by more than 100,000 votes. It was a landslide nationwide. Hughes defeated his opponent by more than 400,000 votes. It was a massive landslide in Iowa, too. It also was the first year the Legislature had started to be reapportioned. So a huge majority of Democrats came in both the House and Senate.

I always recall this little thread: The General Assembly was so confused after the 1962 Supreme Court decision because it was being forced by the courts to come up with a plan. It couldn't even figure out how to divide Polk County into five Senate districts, so all five Senate candidates in Polk County ran at-large. That means that all ten House members ran at-large. Just like that, you had fifteen legislators from Polk County who all ran at-large and were all elected from Polk County as Democrats. Things like that happened all over Iowa. It took most of the rest of the '60s to come up with a way to deal with all of this in terms of how to redistrict and how to get to one man – one vote.

I served in the General Assembly with state senators and state representatives who had been elected back in the 1950s and came from the old system. There was no professional agency at the General Assembly to even write the bills or handle the budget. It was all done by legislators in their heads and their secretaries, who often would be their wives or other women recruited from the local area, and they would write the bills. It meant that the Iowa Code, which is a compilation of legislative bills over 140 years, was always filled with errors and inconsistencies.

When I got there, a bill was passed every year called the code editor's bill. The code editor would be a fairly prominent job in state government. The code editor collected evidence from around the state of errors and inconsistencies. Then the code editor would assemble a bill that corrected the inconsistencies. Theoretically, the code editor's bill was not controversial. It would simply correct grammar, gender, and other things like that.

Later in my twenty-four years as state senator, the General Assembly started having two code editor's bills: one that dealt with more controversial subjects and one that was noncontroversial. It illustrated the idea that everything being printed had all kinds of potential for flaws. Not that a modern electronic system doesn't have flaws. It does.

The community college districts are another example of Iowa moving forward in 1965 when Hughes was governor. In 1965 the state made sure every county in Iowa fit into one of sixteen districts. Each district then was authorized to get a community college, which was two years of post-high school education. The community colleges concentrated theoretically on the kinds of things people did around the farm, modern machinery, and a more sophisticated system of roads. Community colleges were a big achievement of the Hughes era. Some community colleges existed before Hughes was elected governor. There was a very prominent one in Cedar Rapids called Kirkwood Community College. Some simply took the change in the state law and became a much bigger presence. In other places, community colleges were started from scratch.

Area education agencies were established later to support school districts and provide services to students with disabilities. At the time, there were six hundred or more school districts in Iowa. For example, the area education agency in Davenport covered four or five counties with as many as twenty-two or twenty-three school districts. My wife, Mardi, became the coordinator for a project called the Parent-Educator Connection at the area education agency in Bettendorf. She worked for the better part of 16 1/2 years at the Mississippi Bend Area Education Agency. She tried to help the parents of students with disabilities deal with the professionals who worked in special education. The area education agency employed people who were highly educated with doctorates in such fields as psychology and learning disabilities.

The state also moved forward on alcohol and drug abuse assistance. The 1965 General Assembly made the courts more modern, too.

Lt. Gov. Bob Fulton was elected with Harold Hughes in 1964 and again in 1966. Fulton had been a state senator and was a very key player for Hughes. He knew the issues and how to get the legislators to vote for the bills. County interests identified Fulton as being part of the change that happened in the 1960s, and the counties held that against him. I knew Fulton well. He was our candidate for governor in 1970 and Hughes sent me out to Iowa to work on the campaign, so I traveled with Fulton. One of the things held against him was he somehow was lowering the power of the counties by fostering these bigger districts. To my knowledge, Fulton never proposed eliminating counties. But the counties feared elimination of the counties.

———

It may have been very hard to get anything done in the period following World War II through the 1962 Supreme Court decision Baker vs. Carr, but some things did get started. For instance, President Eisenhower proposed an interstate highway system comparable to the German Autobahn that he saw in Europe in World War II. He did not propose it in his first term from 1952 to 1956. He only proposed it after he was reelected in 1956.

When I was in high school and college, the interstate highway system was connected from the Chicago area to the Rock Island/Moline area. I can remember driving across the bridge at Davenport going north a little way and picking up the interstate highway system and driving east on the interstate. It happened before Davenport was connected going west to Iowa City or Iowa City to Des Moines or Des Moines to Council Bluffs.

When Hughes became governor in 1963, the system still was not very well developed, meaning opened up. In 1966 John Hansen lost his reelection bid for Congress from southwest Iowa. He was a close ally of Hughes, and Hansen became chairman of the board that governed the Iowa Highway Commission. The highway commissions were imposed on state governments by Eisenhower's interstate highway program. In Washington, D.C., Eisenhower did not have a high opinion of anyone running for elective office. His impression of state legislatures and congress was not all that positive.

In order to get the interstate highway system built in a fair and honest way, the governor had to appoint a highway commission with citizens as members and a director, the idea being if Illinois was going to run a highway over to the Iowa border, Iowa should meet that highway at the border and keep on going. When you look back on these things, they seem quite logical. But getting them done is hard.

So I had long conversations with Hansen two or three times. It had to do with the diagonal that exists to this day when you drive from Des Moines to Minneapolis. You drive north out of Des Moines on Interstate 35 to Fort Dodge. Then just north of Fort Dodge you veer to the right and cut across on an angle on your way to Mason City. Then you more or less go straight out of Mason City up to the Minnesota border and to the Twin Cities.

That diagonal in 1968 still was enormously troublesome. Why? Because the farm fields are laid out on a north/south grid and to do a diagonal, you're going to cut across farm fields that are laid out on a grid. The end result for the farmer whose farm is divided by a diagonal interstate highway is he might have an eighty-acre plot with forty acres on one side of the interstate and forty acres on the other side. So it wasn't as easy to farm with tractors and machinery as a nice square or rectangular plot.

So Hansen had a job to do to chart a course across that portion of Iowa for the diagonal. They could do it. I have no doubt in 2019 that if you knew who to talk to in these various counties, there would still be people very upset about the diagonal although it happened in 1967 and 1968.

I have another example, although it's not in Iowa. Sometime in the 1980s I was invited to go to a big conference at the state capitol in Florida. I arranged to go down one day early and spend a day in the Florida state Senate. A state senator with jurisdiction over highways described how the bottom part of Florida has three counties across. That three-county model works three, four, or five times as you go down to the southern end of Florida. The senator said trying to get those counties to agree to state-authorized highways that would go across from this county to the next county to the next county was still impossible in the 1980s. He said to me, "I understand in Iowa you can get this done. We've been unable to get it done in Florida."

When Hughes was elected governor for the first time, the state of Iowa's contribution to the six hundred-plus school districts around Iowa was very small. State funds provided 2 percent of the school districts' budgets. By 1968 Hughes had raised that to 8 percent because he had worked in the '65 session especially to provide some state funding for local school districts. Today, we still have more than three hundred school districts in Iowa after considerable school consolidation.

What's the point? One point is the school districts around the state were very appreciative of the effort Hughes had made on their behalf to allow some state funds to go to support local school districts. Based on that, a very significant number of highly visible public school advocates endorsed Hughes for Senate in the 1968 campaign. They were a very key player in winning the Senate seat against Stanley.

It was a bad year to run as a Democrat for the Senate in 1968. Hubert Humphrey lost Iowa to Richard Nixon for the presidency by something like 142,000 votes. Hughes' margin was a very slender 6,415 votes over Stanley. Without the support of the school constituency, we never would have won that election. They were not the only constituent group responsible for helping win that election, but they certainly deserve credit in a big way. The other two constituencies that helped enormously were the two universities: the University of Iowa in Johnson County and Iowa State University in Story County. Both of those counties increased their margins for Hughes in a big way in the 1968 Senate race.

Something else happened in 1968 that had a great significance: the primary race for governor on the Republican side. There were three candidates for governor on the Republican side: Bob Ray, a Des Moines lawyer, and two others, Bob Beck from Centerville and Donald Johnson from West Branch. Ray never would have won that primary if he only had one opponent. The other two split the vote of the small towns and rural areas. It was a big hurdle for a Des Moines lawyer who was called a divorce lawyer, which didn't play well with some of the Republican constituency. But he won with a little more than 40 percent of the vote in the primary and became the GOP nominee.

When Ray came into office in 1969, the state was still grappling with taking state funding and putting it into local school districts. Sometime after 1970, Ray and the Republicans came up with the school aid formula, which is still used today. The formula relates to the number of students in a district and how much state money will go into the school district. As you go from 1970 to the 1980s and into the '90s, the state provided more than 60 percent of the budget in some school districts. And that endures to this day. Over the years that represents an enormous shift in how the state plays in local school districts. So Gov. Ray always got credit for that. From his perspective, the school districts were not grateful enough. They always wanted more.

A friend of mine named Bill Hedlund and a lawyer, Serge Garrison, now deceased, were part of the first Legislative Services Agency in the early 1960s. From talking to legislators I learned that in the early 1960s whoever was the secretary of an Iowa senator or a member of the House would be the one who drafted the bill. The legislator would say to "draft me a bill that does this or that," and the secretary would print something up, and then that's what got passed by the General Assembly. Garrison and Hedlund tried to make sure the bills that were drafted would actually fit into the Iowa Code and bring some order to the process.

One of the first agencies that was set up was the Legislative Services Bureau. They would hire some people who had just gotten out of law school and others to draft bills for the General Assembly. They got that off the ground by 1965. It made the process more professional.

When I was elected to the Iowa Senate in 1978, there still was a Legislative Services Bureau and a Legislative Fiscal Bureau. Later they were combined into a Legislative Services Agency with a fiscal bureau and a services bureau. That exists to this day. The services bureau drafts the bills and amendments, and the fiscal bureau handles the budget and taxation issues.

There is a lawyer at the Legislative Services Agency named Ed Cook. Cook has been in charge of writing approximately three versions of reapportionment bills going back to 1990. He is one of several very professional, very qualified people who are nonpartisan. The Senate Democrats and Senate Republicans have their own partisan staffs; the House Democrats and House Republicans have their own partisan staffs. There are seven or eight people who are employed year-around and look at the issues from the angle of the interest groups, advocacy groups, and other people around the state who want to get something done. They also look at how it affects the legislators trying to figure out how to get it done, and whether anything needs to be modified.

The partisan staff has to look at it from the angle of the legislators, which is a very profound way to deal with things. It's profound because if you're a legislator from Davenport as I was, you have a big interest in such things as the Mississippi River and exports/imports as they relate to the Mississippi River as well as population issues as they relate to the schools in the city and nearby suburbs. You need a staff person year-around at the General Assembly with a partisan viewpoint who can help you weigh how this issue is going. Often times when one person wants something, someone else is going to be hurt by what the other person wants.

That's a different calculation than the Legislative Services Agency with Ed Cook and his counterparts make. Their job is to hear you say what you're going to do, and then draft language that is understandable to the courts, the governmental agencies that have to deal with the bill once it's passed, and citizens who want an honest version of the bill. Citizens don't want tricks in the bill that no one knows about. A lot of people would wonder why a Legislative Services Agency and the partisan staff are necessary, but they do two very different functions from the viewpoint of legislators. The partisan staff can help legislators deal with the press. To sell something to the citizens, legislators have to tell a story to the press that's understandable. That's not the job of the Legislative Services Agency.

The Legislature polished the approach again and again between 1970 and 1990. The general approach was to have one person-one vote, and to divide the state into one hundred house districts and fifty Senate districts. That general approach has endured since approximately 1970. Former state Sen. Michael Gronstal, a brilliant legislator, made this point: Sometime after 1970, something was added to how reapportionment was done. You divide big cities before small cities. You respect municipal boundaries to the degree you can. The result of that is if you look at the Iowa House and then the Iowa Senate, you will find every small town that adjoins a city like Des Moines is not divided, but Des Moines is divided. So you wind up with a real bias toward small town districts at the House and Senate.

In the Iowa Senate, you'll have several senators who are elected in cities such as Des Moines, Cedar Rapids, and Davenport. Then you'll have several legislators who represent the rural and small town area around the city. That model is repeated again and again around Iowa. There are some rural districts that are very big. At one time, there were four Senate districts across southern Iowa: one in the southwest corner, one west of Interstate 35, one east of I-35, and one more in the southeast corner in order to have approximately sixty thousand people in the Senate district. It's the willingness of the suburban legislators to sometimes vote with the cities and sometimes vote with the great big rural districts that charts the future of Iowa. That explains all sorts of things that happen.

There's a Republican state senator now from eastern Polk County. His election seven or eight years ago illustrated he knows what he's doing. He ran television ads in Des Moines that said something like this: "I'm running for the Iowa Senate from a district in northeast Polk County and my grandparents came from Grundy County [or some other rural county]." I would laugh and say, is that a persuasive message – where your grandparents came from? When I ran in Scott County, I didn't say my grandma came from Bernard. It seemed to be so suggestive of this idea: He knew what his district was like and his district had a bunch of people who came from other parts of Iowa and gathered around the three metropolitan areas.

That's my version of modern Iowa: there are three metropolitan areas – Des Moines/Ames, Cedar Rapids/Iowa City, and Davenport/Bettendorf/Muscatine. If you live within forty miles of one of those metropolitan areas, you have a very modern lifestyle with modern health care, education, and shopping opportunities. But if you live one hundred miles away, it's a lot different. Younger people are moving from one hundred miles away to these metropolitan areas, and that's where the legislative districts are because that's where the people are. When a legislator runs an ad about his grandparents coming from Grundy County, he's selling a persuasive message to people who don't think of themselves as coming from Des Moines or Polk County.

ACKNOWLEDGMENTS

Here's a word of thanks from Pat Deluhery at the end of this project.

———

Co-author Steve Dunn: patient. This project took approximately sixteen months of Steve's life. He truly embodies the best of American journalism. He listens, then accurately recounts what he has heard. This book is the result of an extraordinary effort by a very good journalist. Thank you, Steve.

———

Tom Vilsack: U.S. secretary of agriculture, governor, state senator, and mayor. Tom helped me on issues, campaigns, and major decisions.

———

Frank Wessling: journalist. Frank guided my efforts in 1978 and for many more years.

———

The late Bill Hutchins: state senator. Hutch put different issues in my path and then allowed me to negotiate solutions. Sens. Wally Horn and Mike Gronstal, too.

Don Moeller and Ed Rogalski: St. Ambrose University. Their decisions made possible my two careers in politics and higher education.

Debbie O'Leary, Theresa Kehoe, and Robyn Mills: very talented Iowa Senate staff, who guided my legislative efforts.

Dan Looker, Mardi Deluhery, Kirstin Martin, Jeff Dunn, and Paula Barbour: Thanks for your valuable help as we finish this project.

Sheila Deluhery: My sister, who cared for our children when Mardi campaigned and who could always be counted on when we needed a laugh.

There are so many others who I could and should mention. Maybe I'll write another book!

To our readers: This is how I remember it, as Tom Kennelly said, "You might remember it differently."

If you don't like what I wrote, be sure to tell someone else. It might help sales! Mistakes in detail are my responsibility. If there are spelling and printing mistakes, blame the twenty-first century word processing mechanical systems.

Finally, I ended a lot of speeches by quoting an old politician: "Thems my views … and if you don't like 'em … I'll change 'em."

ABOUT THE AUTHORS

Author Pat Deluhery worked on Gov. Harold Hughes' successful campaign for the U.S. Senate before moving to Washington, D.C. to work in Hughes' office from 1969 to 1975. He then worked eight months in Sen. John Culver's office and returned to St. Ambrose College in Davenport, Iowa as an assistant professor in economics and business. He was elected to the Iowa Senate in 1978 and continued to teach at St. Ambrose each year in the summer and fall until December 2002. He and his wife, Mardi, have three daughters and three grandchildren.

Pat Deluhery

Co-author Steve Dunn has written four player biographies and two game stories for the Society for American Baseball Research (SABR). He retired and moved to Des Moines in 2014 after four decades as a sports writer, reporter and managing editor for daily and weekly newspapers. A graduate of Bradley University in Peoria, Illinois, he and his wife, Cindy, have two daughters and three grandchildren.

Steve Dunn

www.ingramcontent.com/pod-product-compliance
Lightning Source LLC
Chambersburg PA
CBHW051401290426
44108CB00015B/2104